Representative Democracy in America

INSTRUCTIONAL GUIDE

Representative
DEMOCRACY
in America
Voices of the People

Center for Civic Education
5145 Douglas Fir Road, Calabasas, CA 91302
818.591.9321   www.civiced.org

Representative Democracy in America

VIDEO SERIES INSTRUCTIONAL GUIDE

A Six-Part Video Series and Instructional Guide

A Project of the Alliance for Representative Democracy

Center for Civic Education
Trust for Representative Democracy /
  National Conference of State Legislatures
The Center on Congress at Indiana University

Developed and produced by the Center for Civic Education
and funded by the U.S. Department of Education under the
Education for Democracy Act approved by the United States
Congress. Contents do not necessarily represent the policy
of the Department of Education, nor should endorsement
by the federal government be assumed.

   08 07 06   01 02 03

ISBN: 0-89818-199-2

CONTENTS

Dear Teacher:

It is with great pleasure that I introduce *Representative Democracy in America: Voices of the People*. This video series consists of six programs designed to inform middle and high school students about representative democracy—the foundation for our American political system.

The series was developed with the involvement of students, teachers, scholars, and other educational leaders to help students understand the essential elements of representative democracy and encourage their commitment to become responsible participants in it.

Representative Democracy in America is a national project designed to reinvigorate and educate Americans on the critical relationship between government and the people it serves. The project introduces citizens, particularly young people, to the representatives, institutions, and processes that serve to realize the goal of a government of, by, and for the people.

The Center for Civic Education has joined with the Center on Congress at Indiana University and the Trust for Representative Democracy/ National Conference of State Legislatures to implement this five-year project with funding from the U.S. Department of Education.

We appreciate your interest in the series and your willingness to use all or part of it in your classroom. We hope you will forward to us any comments or suggestions regarding the strengths and weaknesses of the project. We are particularly interested in receiving anecdotal information about the impact of the program on students' understanding, skills, attitudes, and behaviors.

We hope you find the series an effective means of developing a more profound understanding and appreciation of representative democracy in your students, and that they come away with a sense that their voices can be heard.

Sincerely,

Charles N. Quigley
EXECUTIVE DIRECTOR

Overview of Instructional Package

The video series and instructional guide are designed primarily for high school students, though various elements may be appropriate for middle school or even upper elementary students.

OVERVIEW OF COMPONENTS

Introduction

The six programs, each dealing with an aspect of representative democracy, are designed to be used as a complete series, but may also be used independently. Each program is 15–20 minutes long, and you may choose to show the entire program or particular segments. It may be useful to stop the program at various points to engage students in discussion on certain issues. To facilitate such discussion, the programs are divided into chapters, and a chapter menu precedes each program.

Instructional Package

The instructional package includes:

➤ A series overview and six video programs

➤ *Representative Democracy in America Instructional Guide* with
  • a synopsis of each program
  • two lesson plans for each program
  • a bibliography for each program
  • a set of correlations to the text of the Center's major curricular program, **We the People: The Citizen and the Constitution**

➤ **Series Overview**   TOTAL RUNNING TIME (TRT) 20:00
A reference for the material covered in each program

➤ **Program 1**   TRT 20:00
What Are the Roots of Representative Democracy?

➤ **Program 2**   TRT 16:30
What Are Federalism and the Separation of Powers?

➤ **Program 3**   TRT 15:20
What Are the Roles of Representatives, Executives, and Justices in Our Democracy?

➤ **Program 4**   TRT 19:00
Who Are Our Representatives and How Do We Choose Them?

➤ **Program 5**   TRT 19:40
How Do Representatives Work to Represent Us?

➤ **Program 6**   TRT 19:50
What Are Citizens' Roles in Representative Democracy?

Synopses

A brief synopsis of each program describes in detail the content of that program and its approach to the topic. The synopses provide a quick overview so that you can discern how individual programs, and the series as a whole, can best be used in your classroom.

Lesson Plans

Two lesson plans are provided for each of the six programs. Both sets of plans provide a basic approach to addressing the topics presented and can be adapted as appropriate to the needs of the class. Additional activities are also included in each plan.

Bibliography

There is a bibliography for each program. Designed to serve primarily as a resource for the teacher, items in the bibliography may sometimes be useful for students as well.

Correlations

The correlations suggest how the video series can best be used in conjunction with the Center's curricular program **We the People: The Citizen and the Constitution**, which is designed to enhance students' understanding of our constitutional democracy and help them identify the contemporary relevance of the Constitution and the Bill of Rights.

The correlations indicate which units and lessons of the *We the People* text are most appropriately taught in conjunction with each program of **Representative Democracy in America**. However, the video series also includes important concepts of representative democracy not explored in the *We the People* text.

Synopses

What Are the Roots of Representative Democracy?

Introduction

This initial program introduces the series by providing a brief history of the origins and evolution of some of the fundamental ideas that influenced the Framers of the U.S. Constitution when they created our system of representative democracy in 1787.

Ancient Greece, the Roman Republic, and Renaissance Italy

The story begins in Athens in the fifth century BCE, where the minority of the population that qualified for citizenship participated directly in governing the Athenian city-state (direct democracy).

From Athens, the viewer is introduced to the age of the Roman Republic, when Rome was ruled by a senate composed of the representatives of wealthy families. Later, however, after much social strife, representation was extended to ordinary citizens (classical republicanism).

The program next examines the Florentine Republic of Renaissance Italy. During this period, Florence was ruled by a representative council of the aristocracy and an assembly of all men capable of bearing arms (Italian Renaissance republicanism).

The Reformation

The story then moves to sixteenth-century Reformation Europe to examine the political consequences of the Christian doctrine of universal human equality in the eyes of God. The practice of church governance followed by many Reformation Protestant congregations was later to influence the rise of democratic government among early American colonists. At the heart of this form of governance was the idea of entering into covenants—agreements created by congregation members who mutually consented, in the presence of God, to form a self-governing community. The Mayflower Compact of 1620 is an example of such a covenant (covenants, social compact, consent, self-government).

Developments in England, beginning with the Magna Carta

The program shifts to developments in England, from the signing of the Magna Carta in 1215 to the eighteenth century. Among the ideas that evolved during this period were the rule of law and limited (constitutional) government, which led to the emergence of Parliament, a legislative body composed of two chambers: the House of Lords, representing the aristocracy, and the House of Commons, whose members were—in theory—democratically elected (representative government).

Locke, Montesquieu, and the Age of Enlightenment

By the end of the seventeenth century, the English philosopher John Locke had set forth the theory that the supreme powers of government lie in the hands of the people (popular sovereignty) and that all persons are born with certain rights, including those to life, liberty, and property (natural rights). He held, furthermore, that the just powers of government are limited by the rights of the people and that, if government abuses its powers, the people have a right to change or abolish that government, even, if necessary, by force (right to revolution).

During the Enlightenment of the following century, the French philosopher Montesquieu advocated dividing the government into legislative, executive, and judicial branches as a means of limiting power for the protection of liberty (separation of powers).

The development of representative democracy in colonial America and the United States

The viewer then learns how these ideas were adapted and shaped in the largely self-governing American colonies, where the seeds of today's representative democracy were taking root. The program describes the structure of American colonial government, followed by an account of how the national government was created, first by the Articles of Confederation and then by the U.S. Constitution.

Finally, the program traces the gradual extension of the right to vote up to the present, culminating in the complete inclusion of groups previously denied suffrage. In the process, the viewer is introduced to significant advancements of representative democracy in the past two centuries of American history. This segment concludes by posing several basic questions about representative democracy.

What Are Federalism and the Separation of Powers?

Introduction

Program 2 introduces the federal system and explores some of the reasons the Framers created such a complex system of governance, with powers distributed among national, state, regional, and local governments, as well as different branches of government at each level. This system can be challenging to citizens, who are often confused about which level or levels of government, and which of its branches or agencies, are responsible for matters of interest to them.

The Framers' plan for Congress

When the Framers met in Philadelphia in 1787, they were aware of problems that had arisen with the first government of the United States, which, under the Articles of Confederation, lacked a strong central government. However, the Framers also understood that a strong central government could lead to an abuse of power. To reduce this potential for abuse, they distributed the powers of government among legislative, executive, and judicial branches, and also between the federal government and the states.

Furthermore, the Framers separated powers within the legislative branch, dividing them between the Senate and House of Representatives. The Senate was created to serve the interests of the states, and the House was conceived of as the "voice of the people." The Framers provided for equal representation of the states in the Senate and proportional representation of the people in the House, enabling the smaller states in the Senate to check the power of the larger states in the House. This division of representation and power provided for an internal system of checks and balances in Congress and was intended to foster deliberation, debate, and compromise to achieve the fair representation of all legitimate interests in decision-making.

The Framers create American federalism

Article I of the Constitution designates Congress as the legislative branch of the United States government. The Framers assigned some powers to the federal government, reserved some for the states, and enabled some powers to be shared. This system is an example of federalism.

The Framers' plan for the executive and judicial branches

Article II established the executive branch, and the Framers selected George Washington to serve as the first president under the new Constitution. In this section, the program briefly examines the basic powers of the executive, including those that enable it to check the legislative branch. The ways in which the role of the president has expanded from its initial conception are also discussed.

Article III sets forth the responsibilities of the federal judiciary. These include the power to act on constitutional issues and, through the power of judicial review, to nullify laws and actions of other branches of government when they violate the Constitution.

Shared powers and checks and balances

The system of power sharing created by the Framers established a dynamic relationship among the three branches of the federal government, so that, throughout history, one branch or the other has sometimes taken center stage. Cooperation and competition between the legislative and executive branches is described, as is the dependence of each branch upon the other as a consequence of their shared powers and the system of checks and balances provided by the Constitution.

Multiplicity of governments and their functions

There are more than 87,000 governments and government agencies in the United States administered by elected officials. Furthermore, governments at state and local levels have legislative, executive, and judicial branches. Some functions are assigned exclusively to only one level of government, while others overlap. For example, only the federal government has the power to make treaties with other nations, but federal, state, and local governments each have the power to tax. Powers typically reserved to the states include public education, public safety, and disaster response.

Increase in the powers of the federal government

Over the years, the power of the federal government has increased in relation to that of state governments. The "power of the purse" not only enables the federal government to support programs within states, but also to exert control over states who want to receive federal tax dollars. For example, the federal government pressured states into setting an age limit of twenty-one for drinking alcohol by making it a condition for states to receive federal highway safety funds.

Advantages and disadvantages of federalism

Some of the advantages of federalism include the latitude that states enjoy to experiment with new policies. This has allowed states to take the leadership in reforms in a variety of areas, including child labor and environmental protection. However, when states firmly resist laws passed by Congress, the federal government has the power to enforce compliance, as it did when Arkansas refused to comply with the Supreme Court decision in *Brown v. Board of Education*.

The program concludes with a discussion of the advantages and disadvantages of the system created by the Framers, and also examines the importance of citizens taking responsibility to help the nation live up to its ideals.

What Are the Roles of Representatives, Executives, and Justices in Our Democracy?

Introduction

Program 3 begins with a visit to the three branches of the federal government in Washington, D.C., and a description of the vital but different role each branch plays. This segment also notes how the separation of powers and the system of checks and balances was established by the Constitution as a means to ensure that power will not be abused.

Relationship between the two houses of Congress and between the legislative and executive branches

The struggle between the houses of Congress, and within each house, to pass or block legislation is briefly portrayed, as is the frequent tug-of-war between Congress and the president. This constant battle is a result of the constitutional design of our governmental institutions—a design that fosters debate, bargaining, the consideration of many positions, and compromise in the formulation of public policies. This institutionalized and channeled conflict also takes place in state and local government.

Differences in the election and terms of office of Congress and the president

The president and vice president are elected by the people through the Electoral College and are responsible for representing and speaking for all of the people. The president and vice president are limited to a maximum of two four-year terms, which gives them a certain urgency in pursuing their objectives. By contrast, there is no limit on the number of terms for members of Congress, giving them more time to accomplish their goals. The federalist system requires that Congress and the president cooperate to create laws, so there is constant negotiating between those two branches, as well within the houses of Congress. The process is similar in state and local governments.

The role of the Supreme Court in the system of checks and balances

The highest court in the land, the Supreme Court, can check the exercise of power by Congress, the executive, and the state governments through judicial review—the power of the Court to nullify laws and actions of other branches of government when they violate the Constitution. Supreme Court justices serve for life, and the power to appoint them is shared between the president, who nominates them, and the Senate, which must confirm nominations. As planned by the Framers, all three branches are in a position to check and balance the powers of the others, and they must constantly negotiate.

History of the struggle between presidents and Congress

The first conflict between a president and Congress occurred when George Washington went to the Senate for approval of a treaty. He was not well received and, as a result, did not return to get direct advice and consent from Congress—nor has any president since. This section examines the following relationships of presidents with Congress:

Woodrow Wilson tried to bully the Senate into ratifying his signature of the Treaty of Versailles, which provided for the creation of a League of Nations. He failed, and the League of Nations proved ineffective without American participation.

Franklin D. Roosevelt was able to get many, but not all, of his New Deal reforms enacted into law. When he tried to change the character of the Supreme Court by adding justices who would support his plans, Congress prevented him from doing so.

Conflicts between Congress and two other presidents, Theodore Roosevelt and George H. W. Bush, are also discussed.

The final point is that, in the ongoing tug-of-war between the branches, sometimes the president wins and sometimes Congress wins, but most often they must compromise.

Congressional power to investigate the operations of the executive branch

Congress has the power to investigate the actions and policies of the executive branch and to make the findings public. The first congressional inquiry took place in 1792, and there have been numerous inquiries since that time. President Lincoln's conduct of the Civil War was the subject of a congressional investigation, and one of the most notable investigations led to the resignation of President Nixon.

Congress is also empowered to impeach and convict judges, cabinet members, and presidents. Two presidents have been impeached, Andrew Johnson and William Clinton, but neither was removed from office.

The system of separated powers and checks and balances devised by the Framers of the Constitution has lasted for more than 200 years, and the viewer is left with the question of what might be done to ensure that our representative democracy continues to work well.

PROGRAM 4

Who Are Our Representatives and How Do We Choose Them?

Introduction

Beginning with Program 4, the format changes with the introduction of a panel of three noted scholars who specialize in the nation's legislative institutions and elections. They are Professors Sarah Binder of George Washington University, Anthony Corrado of Colby College in Maine, and Thomas Mann. The first question addressed by the panel concerns the characteristics and motivations of people who serve in the legislative branches of government.

Two views of representation

The composition of federal and state legislatures does not proportionally reflect the population in terms of age, gender, race, or ethnicity. Is this fair representation? The panel discusses two different views of this question. The first view is that legislatures should be composed proportionally of the people whose interests they are supposed to reflect. This means that women should be present to reflect the interests of women, African Americans to reflect the interests of African Americans, and so forth. The second view is that legislatures need not be so composed, as long as legislators reflect the concerns and values of their constituents. Currently, the prevailing opinion is that it is desirable to have women and racial minorities represented by members of those groups, whereas some segments of society, such as young people, can be adequately represented by others.

Motivations to run for legislative office, the demands of the position, and "professional" and "amateur" legislators

Given the considerable demands made on representatives, why do people run for office? The motives discussed range from ambition to the desire to improve life in communities, states, and the nation.

Traditionally, people who run for legislative office have spent their careers in public service and constitute a professional class of representatives who have worked their way up the political ladder. In recent years, however, more representatives have come from other walks of life. These "amateur" legislators are often prominent in other fields, such as sports, show business, or military service, before turning to politics. Moreover, while some states have professional legislatures with staff that serve almost full time, others have civilian legislatures that meet only a few months a year. This segment questions whether professional or civilian representatives create a stronger democracy.

The importance of political parties

American politics today is structured as a competition between the Democratic and Republican parties. They represent almost all public officials and guide most important public policy decisions. Candidates affiliated with the two major parties have many advantages, which is one reason that few people affiliated with other parties succeed in achieving public office.

Gerrymandering

The section explains the origin and effects of gerrymandering—the design of legislative districts to eliminate competition and ensure the advantage of one party's candidates. The use of computers has facilitated the process of gerrymandering and, as a result, less than ten percent of the nation's 435 congressional districts were truly competitive in the 2004 election.

The panelists suggest that solutions to this problem might include establishing checks on legislatures so they cannot create districts to their particular advantage, granting governors veto power over redistricting, having courts review and approve of plans, and creating nonpartisan commissions to establish electoral districts.

Money in politics

In the last few elections, more than one billion dollars was spent to elect members of the Senate and House of Representatives. The average cost of an election campaign is $4 to 4.5 million for the Senate, $600,000 for the House of Representatives, and as much as $50,000 for a state legislature. As a result, many good people do not have the funds to run for office, while incumbents have a distinct advantage because they are typically better known and have more access to funding and other resources.

Why voters vote as they do

Panelists examine the reasons people vote as they do. Often, voters take the default position—voting for members of their party or for measures their party supports. Since parties represent values and policies that voters either agree or disagree with, this provides a shortcut for making decisions when one is not fully informed about the issues at hand. Independents without a strong party affiliation might base their vote on whether they think their state or the nation is going in the right direction.

Reasons for low voter turnout

Despite efforts to motivate people to vote, turnout for elections is often low. This is particularly true for congressional elections. With the exception of about ten percent of congressional districts, where elections are fiercely contested and turnout is high, there is no real competition for congressional seats, and many people in such districts see no point in voting. The overall result is that congressional elections nationwide have become less competitive than they were in the past, and fewer people are motivated to take part in them.

Motivating young people to take part in elections

People tend not to vote if they feel that politicians don't care about them and their vote doesn't matter. However, people can make a difference if they become a political force that politicians must respond to in order to stay in office—and young people must become informed and work together to develop their political power in order to be heard. There is some evidence of this in recent elections and, as a result, political leaders are becoming more attentive to the needs and interests of the young than they have been in the past.

Does the electoral system work?

Panelists express the opinion that the system does not work as well as it could because, among other things, it is so expensive to run for office, and there is insufficient support for candidates to campaign effectively against incumbents.

Panelists also note that the system of open elections and the requirement for frequent reelection have worked for more than 200 years. There is competition for the presidency, control of Congress, and control of state legislatures and local assemblies. The parties are evenly divided, and if people are dissatisfied, they can vote representatives out of office and replace them with others.

What is not working is this: because so few congressional elections are competitive, most critical decisions for the nation are determined long before election day. The panel concludes that we have a good system but can do much better.

How Do Representatives Work to Represent Us?

Introduction

A major challenge for any representative body is how to best represent the public good. This task is significant for the 535 members of Congress, who must represent the diverse interests of more than 280 million people, and raises a complex question: should Congress be guided by something that a majority of its constituents agree upon, or should it try to represent the interests of all of its constituencies? In many instances, one approach or the other would not serve the public good. This issue and others are addressed by the panel.

Special interests

Panelists turn their attention to the matter of special interest groups and their influence on the legislative process. These groups are often geographically based and represent such constituencies as labor, industry, and the professions, usually through local chapters of state or national organizations. The panelists agree that the term special interests is not useful because of its negative implications; in fact, most people use the term to identify a group of which they are not a member. The panel prefers interest groups, a positive concept that forms the basis of the American political system. In our government, individuals and groups express their interests, and politicians protect those interests by responding to their constituents. Out of this process emerges something acceptable, if not optimal, in public policy.

Representatives' responsiveness to constituents

Members of the House of Representatives are typically very attuned to the broad array of interests among their constituents. This task is extremely challenging given the size of constituencies (approximately 650,000 in 2004) and their diversity. Frequent elections ensure that members of the House stay in touch with their constituents by such means as personal meetings, regular review of local media, and frequent visits to their districts, where they maintain offices and staff and attend community events.

The panel also notes that state legislators may be even more accessible, since most of them reside in their districts.

When problems arise between representatives and constituencies, it is generally not because representatives are inaccessible, but because constituents do not communicate with them and make their voices heard.

The role of legislative staff

Congressional staff typically come from the state or district of the representative for whom they work. Staff should be viewed as extensions of members of Congress, serving as members' "eyes and ears," doing the day-to-day work of their offices, assisting in policymaking, negotiating with staff of other members, and listening to constituents.

How a bill becomes a law

The process by which a bill becomes a law is more complicated than it is portrayed in most textbooks. Although bills may be drafted by various agencies of the executive branch and by various interest groups, most of the work and deliberation takes place in committees in the House and Senate. Much of the initial work is done by staff, as is much of the negotiation within and between the two houses. Political parties are also deeply involved, and numerous other interests may be heard in what is typically a very open process.

The strength of a legislature, as opposed to an executive, is that it has many members and can decentralize—that is, it can divide labor into small groups of elected representatives who specialize in a specific area of concern. These groups meet, listen to constituents and other interests, deliberate with colleagues, and try to fashion well-crafted legislation. This is Congress at its best.

The legislative process gets into trouble when representatives pay attention to fellow partisans instead of constituents and follow party lines without adequately considering alternatives.

Characteristics of good representatives

The panel identifies good representatives as those who engage in genuine discussions with constituents and articulate their own views on issues, report regularly to constituents, and address the needs and interests of their constituents, while also addressing national needs.

Delegate and trustee models of representation

In the delegate model of representation, members act on the views of their constituents regardless of alternatives. In the trustee model, representatives use their judgment to act on behalf of their constituents as well as the public good. This segment suggests that good legislators combine these models judiciously and establish a relationship of trust with their constituents.

More characteristics of good representatives

Good representatives also take an interest in public policy; develop expertise in key issues in their districts; direct attention to matters that must be addressed; reach across party lines to develop support for policies; are willing to confront their institution on issues such as campaign finance reform; and provide a voice for those who typically don't have one.

Representation of constituents who did not vote for their representative

How can the needs and interests of voters who opposed the elected candidate be served? This can be accomplished by members of their party who were elected in other districts, or by legislators in another district who represent these voters' interests. Also, once elected, representatives are constantly searching for more support in the next election, which may make them more open to the concerns of constituents who have opposed them.

Strengths and weaknesses of the legislative process

One panelist suggests that both houses of Congress embody positive and negative aspects of the legislative process. In the House, the majority party rules and typically gets what it wants, while the minority party has little opportunity to offer amendments or debate. In the Senate, there is little control over individual senators who can stop votes and bills, anonymously if they choose. This creates an excess of majority rule in the House and an excess of individual or minority rule in the Senate. As a result, the legislative process can be very slow, which is exactly what the Framers intended, so that limited government and the broadest possible interest of the country would be ensured.

A second panelist agrees that one strength of the legislative process is that nothing gets passed without a very strong majority. However, he also thinks that, too often, legislation favored by a majority is held hostage by a small minority. Such a situation can result in effective legislation becoming too compromised or not being passed at all.

Conclusion

The American system is predicated on the expression of diverse interests through deliberation, debate, and compromise. Some people do not understand this process and react negatively to it, but these elements are essential to the democratic process. Of course, when arguments are superficial, strained, exaggerated, or nonsubstantive, people should be suspicious. But citizens must understand that democracy works only by recognizing that we cannot agree on everything and need to find healthy ways of reconciling our differences and living peacefully together.

What Are Citizens' Roles in Representative Democracy?

Introduction

This section deals with how citizens can take part in the democratic process in order to be well represented. One panelist states that citizens need to be engaged in the political process to the extent that they make the system accountable. A republican form of government only works if citizens are prepared to "fire" the very representatives they have elected, so that politicians know they are vulnerable if they do not fulfill their obligations. For the system to work well, citizens also need to become informed, to vote, and to remain involved between elections.

Motivating young people to participate

Young people often feel that politicians neither pay attention to them nor address issues that concern them. The fact is, politicians tend to pay attention to issues that matter to people who vote. If young people begin to vote in larger numbers than in the past, politicians will pay more attention to their needs and interests. To be effective, young people should take the initiative by identifying the issues that are important to them, then informing themselves about those issues and the actions of their representatives.

The importance of campaigns and elections

Campaigns and elections serve to convey information to citizens that they would not otherwise get; encourage involvement in the political process; and provide a number of means for young people, even those who are not of voting age, to participate.

Representatives and campaign promises

Representatives, particularly members of the House, who face frequent elections, have a clear incentive to be responsive to their constituents and to keep promises made during campaigns. In fact, many citizens are unaware of the great extent to which representatives do keep their campaign promises.

Constituents will usually receive a response if they write to their representative asking what positions he or she has taken on issues of interest. This information enables constituents to track promises and judge for themselves whether their representatives are doing enough. New technologies also provide an easy way to track a representative's record.

The roles of media and lobbying groups in campaigns

To keep adequately informed, citizens cannot rely solely on information from a single media source or a particular lobbying group, and representatives may not always portray their activities accurately. People need to be proactive in gathering reliable information and monitoring the activities of their representatives.

Gridlock

Gridlock is the term used for a stalemate that prevents the government from taking action. Although registered voters nationwide are split nearly evenly among Republicans, Democrats, and other parties or independents, the candidates elected to Congress are overwhelmingly either Republicans or Democrats. As a result, the two major parties are often reluctant to compromise and may fail to consider alternative policies that might better serve the public good. This can cause gridlock. While real differences and debates are healthy and not signs that the system is malfunctioning, citizens should challenge their representatives to find middle ground when stalemate occurs.

Constitutional responsibilities of Congress

The powers of Congress, its place as the first branch of government, and its responsibility to oversee the executive branch are established in Article I of the Constitution. At times, Congress fails to fulfill its duty because of partisanship, the desire to please constituencies, or a majority that defers to a president of the same party. When such trends become apparent, citizens should speak with their representatives, vote, and become active in other ways. It is important to note that when there is low voter turnout, the field is left to the most active partisans, promoting polarization and stalemate.

Importance of voting

If citizens do not speak out, their voices will not be heard. Participation by voting and other means does make a difference. The United States has been in existence longer than any other constitutional democracy in history, but it will continue to endure only if its citizens remain informed, active, and engaged.

Representatives as the voice of the people

When there is strong majority support or consensus among the people for specific solutions to specific problems, legislatures can respond fairly quickly and positively. However, when there are many different views on a particular issue, the lack of consensus is usually reflected in legislatures. Nevertheless, representatives are typically very responsive to their constituents and will try to negotiate differences and reach an agreement.

The program concludes with a brief description of two common alternatives to representative democracy—benign dictatorship and direct democracy, both of which are undesirable. For people devoted to the basic values of democracy, representative democracy is the only reasonable choice, and the challenge for citizens is to make it work as well as possible.

Lesson Plans

What Are the Roots of Representative Democracy?

Program 1 Overview

This program explores the roots of representative democracy by tracing the development of its basic concepts and components throughout history. Democracy, classical republicanism, social contract, limited government, rule of law, and natural rights are but a few of the ideas the Framers used in creating our government. The evolution of these ideas—from fifth century BCE Athens and the Roman Republic through the Italian Renaissance and the Protestant Reformation—is examined, as is the impact of the English and French philosophers of the Enlightenment. The program also discusses the development of these ideas during the last 400 years.

Objectives

By the end of this lesson students should be able to

➤ define each of the Terms to Know

➤ trace the historical roots of representative democracy as practiced in the United States today

➤ contrast the difficulties of governing a large, diverse country with that country's need to protect the rights of its population

➤ compare the strengths and weaknesses of representative democracy

➤ evaluate the system of representative democracy with regard to its ability to protect rights, be inclusive of the population, provide opportunities for citizen involvement, and be flexible and enduring

Terms to Know

aristocracy	popular sovereignty
Articles of Confederation	Preamble
bicameral legislature	Protestant Reformation
checks and balances	public good
consent of the governed	Renaissance
covenant	representative democracy
democracy	representative government
direct democracy	republic
limited government	right to revolution
Magna Carta	rule of law
Mayflower Compact	self-government
natural rights	separation of powers

Materials Needed

➤ Program 1: What Are the Roots of Representative Democracy?

➤ Chalkboard, flip chart, or overhead transparencies

➤ A transparency of the focus questions (or student copies) p. 30

➤ Desert Island Activity Sheet (p. 32)

Estimated Time

90 minutes of class time

LESSON PLAN

Introduce the Lesson

To begin, use the Desert Island activity (p. 32). It will spark interest and discussion that links directly to the topic covered in the lesson.

After the groups have created their governments, have them explore the following questions:

- ➤ Why did your group create the system it did?
- ➤ What are the benefits of your plan?
- ➤ What are the possible problems of your plan?
- ➤ Where did you get your ideas?

Transitional Point

Ask the groups to share their answers with the class.

Ask the students the following questions to provide a transition to the program:

- ➤ How does the system your group created compare to the system we currently live under?
- ➤ Where did the Founders get their ideas for creating a system of government?

Place the answers on the board, flip chart, or overhead projector.

View the Program

Focus Questions: Have the students answer these questions as they watch the program:

- ➤ In a country as vast as the United States, how can our voices be heard?
- ➤ How can we be sure that our government does what it is supposed to do?
- ➤ Does representative democracy protect our rights?
- ➤ What are the strengths and weaknesses of representative democracy?

> What is the difference between who can vote today and who could vote in Athens, Rome, and the United States when it first became a nation? What might be the advantages and disadvantages of who can vote today compared with who could vote in the past?

Critical Thinking Exercise

After viewing the program, have the students return to their original groups from the Desert Island activity. While in these groups, they should compare their responses from the Transitional Point with what they now know.

Conclude the Lesson

Have the students remain in their groups and restate Benjamin Franklin's quote as the question:

> If we want this representative democracy to last, what do we need to do to keep it?

Ask the students to answer the question, then have them share their responses with the class.

Supplemental / Additional Activities

1 Play Jeopardy with Terms to Know and historical figures mentioned in the program.

2 Have the students compare a system of government created within the last five years, by any country in the world, with the system created by the Founders.

3 Have the students trace the evolution of a system of government created approximately ten years ago, then compare it with the evolution of our system.

4 Have an in-class debate on the validity of a representative democracy.

5 Have the students research other forms of government, and then have a debate on which one is best.

DESERT ISLAND ACTIVITY SHEET

Prior to the Activity

Divide the class into four or five groups. Assign each member of the group a task (e.g., recorder, reporter, timer, facilitator, leader, etc.), depending on the number of students in the group. You can also assign each member a character. Once the students are set, describe the scenario below.

Scenario

You and your colleagues were on a pleasure cruise when an unexpected and violent storm threw the ship off course. Now, you are all shipwrecked on a desert island. The island is uninhabited but has plenty of resources and can be inhabited. There were approximately 300 people on board the ship. Most have survived. There is no expectation of rescue.

The members of your group have been selected to set up a plan of action. Your task is two-fold:

➤ Create a simple plan of action to deal with immediate problems like health issues, food, etc.

➤ Create a plan of government that will facilitate the survival of the population in the future.

Be prepared to share your plans with the class.

Objectives

By the end of this lesson students should be able to

➤ define each of the Terms to Know

➤ trace the expansion of suffrage in the evolution of representative democracy

➤ explain the relationship between limited government and
  - the separation of powers
  - protection of individual rights
  - checks and balances

➤ identify the strengths and weaknesses of representative democracy

➤ evaluate representative democracy with regard to its ability to
  - provide a voice for the people
  - protect their rights
  - represent their interests
  - promote citizen involvement

Terms to Know

aristocracy	popular sovereignty
Articles of Confederation	Preamble
bicameral legislature	Protestant Reformation
checks and balances	public good
consent of the governed	Renaissance
covenant	representative democracy
democracy	representative government
direct democracy	republic
limited government	right to revolution
Magna Carta	rule of law
Mayflower Compact	self-government
natural rights	separation of powers

Materials Needed

➤ Program 1: What Are the Roots of Representative Democracy?

➤ One copy per student of Terms to Know (Handout 1b_1, p. 37)

➤ One copy per student of Viewing Questions (Handout 1b_2, p. 38)

➤ Debate Topics (p. 39)

➤ Four copies per student of Debate Score Sheet (Handout 1b_3, p. 40)

Estimated Time

90 minutes of class time

LESSON PLAN

Introduce the Lesson

Before viewing the program, ask the students the following questions to determine the depth of their knowledge of representative democracy.

> ➤ What type of government does the United States have?
> ➤ Why did the Framers create this type of government?
> ➤ What is the difference between a direct democracy and a representative democracy?
> ➤ Who should have the right to elect representatives? Why?
> ➤ Where did the basic ideas underlying the government of the United States come from?
> ➤ What are the basic purposes of the government?

Explain that Program 1 will begin to answer these questions as well as the Viewing Questions (p. 38).

View the Program

> ➤ Give each student a copy of the Terms to Know (Handout 1b_1, p. 37) and the Viewing Questions (Handout 1b_2, p. 38).
> ➤ Ask the students to identify as many of the Terms to Know as they can and to listen for these terms as they watch the program. Tell them that you will go over these terms later.
> ➤ Ask the students to answer the Viewing Questions as they watch the program.
> ➤ After viewing the program, review the terms in Terms to Know and clarify any misunderstandings. Ask the students to keep these terms available for reference.
> ➤ Ask for volunteers to share their answers to the Viewing Questions with the class, then correct any mistakes and elaborate on answers that need to be expanded.

Critical Thinking Exercise

➤ Divide the class into at least three groups, with 4 to 8 students in a group.

➤ Subdivide each group into halves. Designate one half as the affirmative side and one half as the negative side.

➤ Explain that each group is going to debate one of the Debate Topics (p. 39) drawn at random.

➤ Conduct the drawing and then explain the debate rules.

- Each side, affirmative and negative, will have three minutes to present their arguments. The affirmative side shall speak first.

- After a short break each side shall have three minutes to question the other side. The negative side shall question the affirmative side first.

- At the end of this cross-examination period, give the students a few minutes to prepare a one-minute closing argument. The affirmative side shall present its closing arguments first.

➤ Ask the students who are observing to use two copies of the Debate Score Sheet (Handout 1b_3, p. 40) to evaluate each side's performance during the debate.

Conclude the Lesson

Debrief each debate by asking the students who were observers the following questions:

➤ Which side, affirmative or negative, presented the most well-reasoned arguments? Why do you think this is so?

➤ Did either side in the debate overlook any important points? If so, what was omitted?

➤ Were any of the arguments presented fallacious? Which ones were they, and why do you think so?

Conclude the lesson by asking the students this overarching question:

➤ What do we need to do to maintain and improve our representative democracy?

LESSON PLAN

**Supplemental /
Additional Activities**

1   Suppose you live in a congressional district that always elects a representative who belongs to a political party that is different from your own: What are the means available for you to influence that representative? Work with several other members of your class to write a response to this question.

2   Take and defend a position on this statement:

➤ Due to advances in technology, direct democracy is now not only possible but also desirable.

3   Obtain the constitution of an advanced or emerging democracy, then

➤ review the bases upon which representatives are selected in that country

➤ identify the differences between those bases and the bases of representation in the United States

➤ explain what appear to be the advantages and disadvantages of the two systems

Terms to Know

- ➤ aristocracy
- ➤ Articles of Confederation
- ➤ bicameral legislature
- ➤ checks and balances
- ➤ consent of the governed
- ➤ covenant
- ➤ democracy
- ➤ direct democracy
- ➤ limited government
- ➤ Magna Carta
- ➤ Mayflower Compact
- ➤ natural rights
- ➤ popular sovereignty
- ➤ Preamble
- ➤ Protestant Reformation
- ➤ public good
- ➤ Renaissance
- ➤ representative democracy
- ➤ representative government
- ➤ republic
- ➤ right to revolution
- ➤ rule of law
- ➤ self-government
- ➤ separation of powers

HANDOUT 1b_2

Viewing Questions

1 How has the right of citizens to have a voice in their government been expanded since the first Athenian democracy?

2 Explain the relationship between limited government and

   a the separation of powers

   b checks and balances

   c the protection of individual rights

3 What are some of the strengths and weaknesses of representative democracy?

4 How well does our representative democracy provide a voice for the people, represent their interests, protect their rights, and promote citizen involvement?

Debate Topics

Topic One

The government established by our Constitution, with its separation of powers and system of checks and balances, is sufficient to maintain order and protect the rights of individuals.

NOTES

Topic Two

The system of equal representation of states in the Senate and proportional representation by population in the House of Representatives is the best way to ensure that the diverse interests of the people are heard.

NOTES

Topic Three

The United States has at last become a true representative democracy.

NOTES

Debate Score Sheet

Directions

For each criterion, score the strategy on a scale of 1–5, with 5 being the best score. Add the scores for each criterion to determine the total score for the strategy.

SCORE

1 poor
2 fair
3 average
4 above average
5 excellent

▼

DEBATE TOPIC

SIDE

☐ Affirmative

☐ Negative

NOTES

Understanding
To what extent did the participants demonstrate knowledge of the basic issues involved in the topic?

Reasoning
To what extent did the participants' arguments follow logically from reasoned thought?

Supporting Evidence
To what extent did the participants support their positions with historical or contemporary evidence and examples?

Responsiveness
To what extent did participants answer the questions that they were asked?

Questioning
To what extent did the questions participants directed to the other side illuminate the important issues?

Participation
To what extent did most of the participants contribute to their side's presentation?

Total

Scorer's Name

What Are Federalism and the Separation of Powers?

Program 2 Overview

The program begins with a series of questions regarding the number of governments that make up the American federal system, as well as the levels and structures of those governments. This is followed by a brief description of the 1787 Philadelphia Convention and the reasons it was convened. The legislative, executive, and judicial branches of the national government are also described, and the powers of each branch, as delineated in Articles I, II, and III of the Constitution, are identified. Examples of powers given to the national government and those retained by the state governments are provided. The program concludes by explaining that in order to create a system of checks and balances, the Framers distributed powers among the different levels of government and separated powers within each level. The result was the creation of a government that combined power with restraint and provided the people with the right to elect representatives at various levels in order to make their voices heard.

Objectives	By the end of this lesson students should be able to

➤ define each of the Terms to Know

➤ differentiate between the powers of the federal, state, and local governments

➤ compare and contrast the powers of each branch of government

➤ explain the function of checks and balances, and cite both historical and contemporary examples

➤ describe the impact of federalism and the separation of powers on the citizenry

Terms to Know

Articles of Confederation	judicial review
checks and balances	legislative branch
civil unrest	Miranda rights
confederation	override of veto
decentralized	power of the purse
executive branch	reserved powers
federalism	Senate
gridlock	separation of powers
House of Representatives	veto
judicial branch	

Materials Needed

➤ Program 2: What Are Federalism and the Separation of Powers?

➤ Chart paper

➤ Colored markers

Estimated Time

50 minutes of class time

LESSON PLAN

Introduce the Lesson

To begin, ask the students the following question:

➤ In how many ways were you affected by government this morning?

Ask them to share their activities from the time the alarm clock went off to the time they set foot in the school building. Make a chronological list of these activities on the board.

Select several activities from the list and have the students determine what kind of governmental regulation or involvement is associated with each one. There is no need to review every activity to give students the understanding that various levels of government are involved in all that we do.

Transitional Point

Divide the class into groups of four or five. Give each group a piece of chart paper with the following questions written on it:

➤ How many different governments govern us?

➤ How can you tell which government is doing what?

➤ What do these governments do?

➤ What can't these governments do?

Ask the students to brainstorm answers and write them down with a colored marker on the chart paper (4–5 minutes).

Once the students have completed this task, ask each group to share their answers.

View the Program

Ask the students to keep these questions and answers in mind as they view the program.

Critical Thinking Exercise

After viewing the program, ask the students to return to their groups and answer the questions again. They should use a different color marker to record these answers.

Have the groups share their answers and compare them with the answers given before viewing the program.

Conclude the Lesson

While still in their groups, the students should answer two additional questions:

➤ What are the positive aspects of this system of divided power?

➤ What are the negative aspects of this system of divided power?

Have several students share their answers with the class.

Supplemental / Additional Activities

Have the students

➤ keep a record of an entire day's activities and describe the governmental involvement in each one

➤ find stories, using a newspaper or newscast, that reflect examples of federalism, checks and balances, and separation of powers

➤ research an issue that involved judicial review

➤ write a paper on the "new federalism" as defined by the Reagan administration and what has since happened to that new federalism

Objectives

By the end of this lesson students should be able to

➤ define each of the Terms to Know

➤ describe the structure of our federal system of government and identify some of its strengths and weaknesses

➤ explain how the distribution of power among the different levels of government and the separation of powers within each level result in a system of checks and balances

➤ identify some of the powers held by each branch of government and each level of government

➤ evaluate representative democracy with regard to its ability to provide a voice for the people, represent their interests, protect their rights, and promote citizen participation

Terms to Know

Articles of Confederation	judicial review
central government	legislative branch
checks and balances	local government
civil unrest	override of veto
executive branch	power of the purse
federalism	reserved powers
gridlock	Senate
House of Representatives	separation of powers
judicial branch	veto

Materials Needed

➤ Program 2: What Are Federalism and the Separation of Powers?

➤ One copy per student of Terms to Know (Handout 2b_1, p. 53)

➤ One copy per student of Viewing Questions (Handout 2b_2, p. 54)

➤ Rules for Class Feud (pp. 55–56)

➤ One copy per student of Class Feud Survey (Handout 2b_3, p. 57)

➤ One copy per team of Team Tally Sheet (Handout 2b_4, p. 58)

Estimated Time

90 minutes of class time

LESSON PLAN

Introduce the Lesson

Ask the students the following questions to determine the depth of their understanding of federalism.

- ➤ What are the different levels of government in the United States?
- ➤ What is the purpose of having different levels of government?
- ➤ What are the branches of government at each level?
- ➤ Why did the Framers create this system of government?
- ➤ What is this system of government called?

View the Program

- ➤ Give each student a copy of the Terms to Know (Handout 2b_1, p. 53) and a copy of the Viewing Questions (Handout 2b_2, p. 54).
- ➤ Give the students a few minutes to identify as many of the Terms to Know as they can and ask them to listen for these terms during the program. Tell them that you will go over the terms later.
- ➤ Ask the students to answer the Viewing Questions as they watch the program.
- ➤ When the students finish viewing the program, review the Terms to Know and clarify any misunderstandings. Ask them to keep these terms available for reference.
- ➤ Ask the class for volunteers to share their answers to the Viewing Questions. Correct any mistakes and elaborate on answers that need to be expanded.

Critical Thinking Exercise

Preparation steps

➤ Divide the class into two teams, a Red team and a Blue team, and give each student a copy of the Class Feud Survey (Handout 2b_3, p. 57).

➤ Ask each student to identify ten powers that are given to the national government and ten powers that are reserved to the state governments, and to record his or her response on the Class Feud Survey. (Note that students are to work individually.)

➤ When the students complete their surveys, collect them and tally the results for each team on the appropriate Team Tally Sheet (Handout 2b_4, p. 58). These tallies will enable you to create the top-ten lists of powers for each team. (You may want to appoint one student from each team to assist in tabulating his or her team's lists. These students will not be allowed to play the game.)

➤ When all the surveys have been tallied you are ready to begin Class Feud.

➤ Explain the Rules for Class Feud (pp. 55–56). (The above instructions are also included on that page.)

Conclude the Lesson

Concluding steps

➤ When you have finished the game, correct any mistakes that were made by students in listing the powers of the national government and the state governments.

➤ If you did not use the tiebreaker during the game, be sure to point out that some powers belong to both the national government and the state governments.

Debrief this activity by creating a Venn diagram on the board. Label one circle "Powers of the National Government" and label the second circle "Powers Reserved to the States." The area in which the circles overlap represents the powers belonging to both levels of government. Ask the students to create their own diagrams with a correct listing of the powers belonging to the national government, the state governments, and to both levels of government. (You may want to collect these diagrams and use them as an assessment of student understanding.)

**Supplemental /
Additional Activities**

1 Ask the students to write an essay describing the advantages and disadvantages of a federal system of government.

2 Ask the students to contrast a federal system of government with a unitary system and a confederacy.

3 Ask the students to take and defend a position on one of the following statements:

> ➤ A federal system of government is more likely than a unitary system to protect the rights of citizens and provide them with opportunities to participate.

> ➤ A federal system of government is too complex a form of government to be effective in a large and/or populous nation.

Terms to Know

➤ Articles of Confederation

➤ central government

➤ checks and balances

➤ civil unrest

➤ executive branch

➤ federalism

➤ gridlock

➤ House of Representatives

➤ judicial branch

➤ judicial review

➤ legislative branch

➤ local government

➤ override of veto

➤ power of the purse

➤ reserved powers

➤ Senate

➤ separation of powers

➤ veto

HANDOUT 2b_2

Viewing Questions

1 What branches of government are created in Articles I, II, and III of the Constitution respectively?

2 What are some powers granted to the national government?

3 What are some powers retained by state governments?

4 Why are some powers given exclusively to each branch of government?

5 What are some powers that are shared by the three branches of government?

6 What happens when a state refuses to follow a law passed by the national government?

7 Why is an independent judiciary important?

Preparation Steps

> Divide the class into two teams, the Red team and the Blue team, and give each student a copy of the Class Feud Survey (Handout 2b_3).

> Ask each student to identify ten powers that are given to the national government and ten powers that are reserved to the state governments, and to record his or her response on the Class Feud Survey. (Note that students are to work individually.)

> When the students complete their surveys, collect them and tally the results for each team on the appropriate Team Tally Sheet (Handout 2b_4). These tallies will enable you to create the top-ten lists of powers for each team. (You may want to appoint one student from each team to assist in tabulating his or her team's lists. These students will not be allowed to play the game.)

> When all the surveys have been tallied you are ready to begin Class Feud.

> Explain the rules for Class Feud given below.

Class Feud consists of two rounds of play plus a "sudden death," if needed. The rules are as follows:

Round One

1   Each team, Red and Blue, shall designate **five players** to participate in this round.

2   **Flip a coin** to determine which team goes first.

3   The team that goes first will begin by having each of its **five players attempt to identify a distinct power** on their Team Tally Sheet (Handout 2b_4) list of federal (national) government powers. The players may go in any order they wish, but they may not receive help from their teammates.

4   When all five players on the first team have made their guesses, the **five players from the second team** will each attempt to identify **five other distinct powers** on their Team Tally Sheet list of federal government powers. The players of the second team **may not repeat any correct answers** given by the first team.

(Continued on next page)

5   A team is awarded **two points for every correct answer** that a player gives. For example, if four players from the Blue team correctly identify a power that is on their team's list, then the Blue team will earn eight points. Each team can earn a maximum of ten points in round one.

Round Two

1   Each team shall designate **five new players** to participate in this round.

2   The **team that went second** in round one shall go first in round two.

3   Each of the **five new players** on the team going first shall attempt to identify a different power on their Team Tally Sheet (Handout 2b_4) list of top ten powers reserved to the states. Again, they may go in any order, but they may not receive help from their teammates.

4   When the players from this team finish, each of the **five new players** on the second team shall attempt to identify a distinct power on their team's list. They **may not repeat any correct answers** given by the first team.

5   Every correct answer in round two is worth **three points**. Each team can earn a maximum of fifteen points in round two.

6   **Tally the total points** from round one and round two for each team, using the method described above. The team with the most points wins.

Sudden Death

In the event of a tie, each team will select **one player** who will identify a power that is held by both the federal government and the state governments. Both players will **write their answers** on a sheet of paper. If there is another tie, continue the game with two new players until one team wins. If there is no winner after five tiebreaker rounds have been completed, declare the game a draw.

Class Feud Survey

Directions

Complete this survey by identifying ten powers that belong to the federal (national) government and ten powers that belong to the state governments.

➤ Name

➤ Your Team

Powers of the federal (national) government

1

2

3

4

5

6

7

8

9

10

Powers of state governments

1

2

3

4

5

6

7

8

9

10

HANDOUT 2b_4

Team Tally Sheet

Directions

List the most frequently named powers for each level of government, according to the surveys completed by the members of each team. (If fewer than 10 powers are identified, list only the ones that are named.)

➤ Team Name

Powers of the federal (national) government

1 _____

2 _____

3 _____

4 _____

5 _____

6 _____

7 _____

8 _____

9 _____

10 _____

Powers of state governments

1 _____

2 _____

3 _____

4 _____

5 _____

6 _____

7 _____

8 _____

9 _____

10 _____

What Are the Roles of Representatives, Executives, and Justices in Our Democracy?

Program 3 Overview

The three branches of the federal government established by the Constitution are identified at the beginning of this program. The role of each branch is then explored with respect to the separation of powers and system of checks and balances created by the Framers. The relationship between the two houses of Congress is described, as is the relationship between the legislative and executive branches of government, with special attention given to the history of the struggle between presidents and Congress. The program concludes with a description of the powers of Congress to investigate the activities of the executive branch.

Objectives	By the end of this lesson students should be able to

> define each of the Terms to Know

> enumerate the powers of each branch of the federal government

> differentiate between the separation of powers and the system of checks and balances, providing at least two historical and two modern-day examples of each

> discuss the struggles that occur among the three branches of government as they try to maintain the balance of power

Terms to Know

bully pulpit	parliamentary procedures
checks and balances	public policies
electoral college	separation of powers
executive branch	sharing of powers
impeach	treaty
judicial branch	unconstitutional
legislative branch	veto
New Deal	veto override

Materials Needed

> Program 3: What Are the Roles of Representatives, Executives, and Justices in Our Democracy?

> Chalkboard or transparency for the three branches of government

> Directions (Handout 3a_1, p. 66)

> Descriptors/Situations (Handout 3a_2, p. 67)

Estimated Time

90 minutes of class time (two in-class periods), with library time required between the two periods

LESSON PLAN

Introduce the Lesson

To begin this lesson, place an illustration with the names of the three branches of government on the board or screen and ask the students to answer the following question:

➤ Which of these three branches is more powerful and/or important?

Upon completion, have students share their answers out loud. Place the students' answers (with reasons and examples) under each branch on the board or screen. Have students speculate as to which of their choices is correct.

View the Program

Activity: Who is correct?

The students will ultimately try to answer this question after viewing the program.

Keep the chart that the students created on the board. Ask them to determine if any of the reasoning or evidence they offered appears in the program.

You may also suggest that they gather definitions of the Terms to Know while watching the program.

Transitional Point

After viewing the program, ask the students to look at the chart and their previous answers.

➤ Is there a definitive answer to the question: Who is correct?
➤ Did they find any of their reasoning in the program?

Critical Thinking Exercise

Divide the class into six groups. Give each group a copy of the Directions (Handout 3a_1, p. 66) and assign to each group one event or situation from Descriptors/ Situations (Handout 3a_2, p. 67). The groups must investigate the situation assigned and answer the questions on the Directions sheet.

This is an opportunity to integrate a library visit so that the students can conduct research needed to complete the task assigned. The library lesson can include research techniques using websites and/or in-house documents and materials.

Conclude the Lesson

Once the task is completed, each group must share their findings with the rest of the class.

Upon hearing all the presentations, the students should reflect on what they have heard and write a brief essay titled "Where Does the Balance of Power Lie?"

Supplemental / Additional Activities

1   Have the students debate or write a brief position paper on whether they think Supreme Court justices should be elected or restricted to a fixed term of office.

2   Have the students research suggested alternatives to the present term of office of the president. What advantages and disadvantages do the alternatives have?

3   Refer the students to Article I, Section 8, of the U.S. Constitution. Ask them to suggest powers of Congress not included that they believe should be, and powers, if any, that are included but should not be. Students must support their suggestions for each addition and deletion.

Directions

Your group has been assigned a situation in American history in which an issue or conflict arose. In resolving that issue or conflict, one branch of government probably took the lead or, in some instances, caused the problem.

The overarching question you must answer is this:

➤ How does this situation illustrate the concept of checks and balances?

To help you, answer the following questions as you investigate your issue:

1 What branch or branches of government were involved?

2 What led to the issue or conflict?

3 How was it resolved?

4 How does this illustrate the concepts of separation of powers and checks and balances?

Once you have completed this task, share the information with the other groups in class.

Descriptors/Situations

➤ President Franklin D. Roosevelt and court-packing

➤ President Harry S. Truman and the integration of the military

➤ The impeachment of President Andrew Jackson

➤ Suspension of habeas corpus in *Ex Parte Merryman* and/or *Ex Parte Milligan*

➤ Legislative veto and the *Chada* case (*Immigration and Naturalization Service v. Chada* [1983])

➤ Restriction of the Supreme Court's jurisdiction and *Ex Parte McCardle*

➤ President Truman and the seizure of the steel mills (*Youngstown Sheet and Tube Company et al. v. Sawyer* [1952])

➤ The War Powers Act of 1973

➤ The presidency and foreign policy (through *United States v. Curtiss-Wright Export Corporation* [1936] or *Reagan v. Wald* [1984])

Objectives	By the end of this lesson students should be able to

- define each of the Terms to Know
- identify the roles and responsibilities of legislators, executives, and justices in our representative democracy
- explain the importance of the separation of powers and the system of checks and balances

Terms to Know

checks and balances	legislative branch
constituents	override
electoral college	separation of powers
executive branch	shared powers
impeach	term of office
judicial branch	unconstitutional
judicial review	veto

Materials Needed

- Program 3: What Are the Roles of Representatives, Executives, and Justices in Our Democracy?
- One copy per student of Terms to Know (Handout 3b_1, p. 73)
- One copy per student of Powers of Government (Handout 3b_2, p. 74)

Estimated Time

120 minutes in class and, possibly, some additional time outside of class

LESSON PLAN

Introduce the Lesson

Ask the students the following questions to determine how much they know about the structure of our federal government, the separation of powers, and the system of checks and balances that have sustained our representative democracy.

- What document created the structure of our federal government?
- Our federal government consists of how many branches? What are they?
- What is the essential role of each branch of the federal government?
- How similar to or different from the structure of the federal government are the structures of state governments?

Explain that **Program 3** will answer these questions and others about the responsibilities of legislators, executives, and justices.

View the Program

- Give each person a copy of Terms to Know (Handout 3b_1, p. 73) and Powers of Government (Handout 3b_2, p. 74).
- Give the students a few minutes to identify as many of the Terms to Know as they can, then tell them to listen for these terms during the program. Let them know that you will go over the terms with them later.
- As they watch the program, ask the students to list powers belonging to the legislative, executive, and judicial branches in the proper columns on the Powers of Government handout.

➤ After viewing the program, review the Terms to Know with the students and clarify any misunderstandings. Ask them to keep these terms available for reference.

➤ Ask for volunteers to share their Powers of Government lists with the class and compile a comprehensive list on the board.

➤ Use the comprehensive list to illustrate the powers that are separated among the three branches of government and those that are shared by more than one branch.

➤ Ask the following questions:

- Why did the Framers of the Constitution separate the powers of government?

- Why did the Framers decide that some powers should be shared?

Critical Thinking Exercise

➤ Divide the class into three groups of approximately equal size. Assign the role of legislative branch to the first group, executive branch to the second group, and judicial branch to the third group.

➤ Ask each group to develop as many arguments as it can for increasing the power of its branch in order to make government run more efficiently and effectively in the twenty-first century.

➤ Ask each group to prepare a defense against the charge that "a change in the balance of power will lead to the abuse of power by its branch of government."

➤ Give the students fifteen minutes to prepare arguments defending their proposed changes, which they will then present to the entire class. Allow the members of other groups to ask questions after each group has completed its presentation.

LESSON PLAN

Conclude the Lesson

Ask the students to write an evaluation of each group's arguments and defenses. These evaluations should identify the individual strengths and weaknesses of each group's work, as well as those that may be common to all three groups. Conclude the lesson by asking this overarching question:

➤ Does the American system of checks and balances need to be adjusted in order to maintain and/or improve our system of representative democracy?

Supplemental / Additional Activities

1 Ask the students to take and defend a position on one of these statements:

➤ The executive branch has acquired such additional powers as to upset the balance of power among the three branches of government.

➤ The judicial branch has used the practice of judicial activism to make laws outside of its constitutionally given authority.

2 Ask the students to identify an instance in which one branch of government attempted and/or succeeded in exercising its power at the expense of the powers of the other branches.

3 Ask the students to explain how the process of amending the Constitution is an example of federalism and not part of the system of checks and balances within the national government.

Terms to Know

➤ checks and balances

➤ constituents

➤ electoral college

➤ executive branch

➤ impeach

➤ judicial branch

➤ judicial review

➤ legislative branch

➤ override

➤ separation of powers

➤ shared powers

➤ term of office

➤ unconstitutional

➤ veto

Powers of Government	**Directions**
	List below the powers for each branch of government.

▼ Legislative

1 _____

2 _____

3 _____

4 _____

5 _____

6 _____

7 _____

8 _____

9 _____

10 _____

▼ Executive

1 _____

2 _____

3 _____

4 _____

5 _____

6 _____

7 _____

8 _____

9 _____

10 _____

▼ Judicial

1 _____

2 _____

3 _____

4 _____

5 _____

6 _____

7 _____

8 _____

9 _____

10 _____

Who Are Our Representatives and How Do We Choose Them?

Program 4 Overview

A panel of three scholars discusses the characteristics of the officials who represent us at the national and state levels of government. The panelists offer insight into what motivates an individual to seek public office, and they examine the role of political parties in determining candidates. The scholars also provide information regarding the impact of gerrymandering and money on the outcome of elections in America. In addition, voter behavior and motivation are described, and their impact on those seeking office is explored. Finally, the panelists provide their opinions on the effectiveness of the electoral system in the United States.

Objectives

By the end of this lesson students should be able to

- define each of the Terms to Know
- discuss the impact of political parties on the election process
- compare and contrast the two views of representation
- explain the effect of partisanship on the legislative process
- explain the importance of young peoples' participation in the legislative process

Terms to Know

bipartisan	paradox
checks and balances	partisan
citizen legislator	professional legislator
constituents	redistrict
gerrymandering	salamander
incumbent	

Materials Needed

- Program 4: Who Are Our Representatives and How Do We Choose Them?
- Directions for Teachers for the Who Are They? activity (p. 82)
- Directions for Teachers for the Jigsaw, a cooperative learning strategy (p. 83)
- Task Assignment Cards (pp. 84–85)

Estimated Time

90 minutes of class time

LESSON PLAN

Introduce the Lesson

Begin the lesson by posing the following question to the students:

➤ Would you run for political office? Why or why not?

Give them a few minutes to write down their answers, which they will then share. Record their answers on the board under the two categories: "Why I would run for political office" and "Why I would not run for political office."

Transitional Point

Prepare for the activity as described in the Directions for Teachers for Who Are They? (p. 82).

Have the students identify the people in the pictures you have gathered by name, occupation, or anything else they can think of. Place each photo into either a "known" or an "unknown" pile based on the students' answers, then identify those people the students did not know.

Pick up all the photos in the "unknown" pile and ask the class:

➤ If we don't know who these people are, how did they get elected?

Transitional Point

This is a cooperative learning strategy, as described in the Directions for Teachers for the Jigsaw (p. 83).

PHASE ONE OF THE JIGSAW
Set up home groups. The ultimate objective of the home group is to answer the focus question:

➤ How effective and efficient is the U.S. election process?

View the Program

As the students view the program, they should keep in mind the individual task they were assigned in the home group.

Critical Thinking Exercise

PHASE TWO OF THE JIGSAW
After viewing the program, set up the expert groups and allow the students to complete their tasks.

PHASE THREE OF THE JIGSAW
The students return to their home groups where they will, as a group, answer the focus question.

Conclude the Lesson

Each group will share its answers with the rest of the class.

Supplemental / Additional Activities

1 Have the students create a short survey and set up an interview with one of their local representatives such as a council member, assemblyperson, or state senator.

2 Have the students illustrate the development and evolution of political parties from the Civil War to the present.

Who Are They?

To complete this activity, gather approximately nine pictures of elected political leaders from magazines, newspapers, etc.

1   The pictures should include at least two prominent national officials who are easily recognizable. The rest of the pictures should be of officials from the students' own state, including senators, members of Congress, state assembly members, state senators, city council members, etc. If pictures of local representatives are difficult to obtain, make placards with the names of such representatives and use these instead of photos.

2   Create two piles: "known" and "unknown."

3   Show the class the pictures or the placards with names. Ask the students to identify the officials and the elected position they currently hold. (Most students should be able to identify the national leaders and perhaps even a senator; however, local representatives are often more difficult to identify, and fewer students will be able to do so.)

4   Place the picture in the corresponding "known" or "unknown" pile. Once all the pictures have been placed, turn to the "unknown" pile and identify the leaders there.

5   When all the "unknown" pictures and placards have been identified, ask the students:

>   If we don't know who these people are, how did they get themselves elected?

6   Try to elicit from students the reasons that these individuals have been able to win elections.

Jigsaw

The Jigsaw is rather complex and is most successful if the students have had prior experience with a cooperative learning strategy.

In the Jigsaw, the students work in two groups.

PHASE ONE
Home Group

1 Divide the class into groups of at least seven members each. Assign roles as you would for any cooperative learning lesson (e.g., leader, timer, facilitator, etc.)

2 Cut out copies of the Task Assignment Cards (pp. 84–85) and give them to the leaders of each group, who will then give one card to each group member.

3 The home groups will ultimately answer the overall focus question:

➤ How effective and efficient is the U.S. election process?

Before they can answer the question, however, the students must complete Phase Two and become "experts" in the area covered on their Task Assignment Cards.

PHASE TWO
Expert Group

The students will now form new groups with those who have the same Task Assignment Cards.

1 Assign roles as you did in Phase One.

2 Together, the students will answer the question on their card and become experts in their specific area. Make sure each member of each group participates and gathers the information necessary to complete the task.

PHASE THREE
Return Home

1 When the expert groups are finished, the students will return to their home groups and share the information they have gathered. The information will be used to answer the focus question above.

2 At the end of the lesson, each home group will hand in a written answer to the focus question.

TASK ASSIGNMENT CARDS

▼   ▼   ▼   PLEASE CUT ALONG DOTTED LINES AFTER YOU HAVE COPIED THE PAGES   ▼   ▼   ▼

Two Views of Representation

1   What are the two views of representation?

2   What are the strengths and weaknesses of each view?

3   Is one view preferable to the other? Why or why not?

Motivation, Demands, and Types of Legislators

1   What motivates people to become legislators?

2   What are the demands of the position?

3   Describe the two types/models of a legislator.

4   Is one type/model preferable? Why or why not?

Gerrymandering

1   What is gerrymandering?

2   How does it affect the election process?

3   What reforms have been suggested for remedying this system? Which would you recommend?

Why Voters Vote as They Do and the Reasons for Low Voter Turnout

1   Why do voters vote as they do?

2   What prevents people from voting?

PLEASE CUT ALONG DOTTED LINES AFTER YOU HAVE COPIED THE PAGES

Motivating Young People to Take Part in Elections

1   How can young people become involved in the election process? As voters? As nonvoters?

2   Why should people participate in a representative democracy?

Money in Politics

1   What is the role of money in the election process?

2   Should the situation be changed? Why or why not?

The Importance of Political Parties

1   What is the role of political parties in the election process?

2   What is the role of political parties in the legislative process?

Objectives

By the end of this lesson students should be able to

➤ define each of the Terms to Know

➤ demonstrate an understanding of the roles that individual motivation, political parties, gerrymandering, money, and voter behavior play in the electoral system

➤ take and defend a position on ways to increase participation by young people in the electoral process

Terms to Know

amateur legislator	independent
bipartisan	nonpartisan
citizen legislator	partisan
electorate	party affiliation
gerrymandering	professional legislator
incumbent	redistricting

Materials Needed

➤ Program 4: Who Are Our Representatives and How Do We Choose Them?

➤ One copy per student of Terms to Know (Handout 4b_1, p. 91)

➤ One copy per student of Viewing Questions (Handout 4b_2, p. 92)

➤ One copy per student of Strategy Evaluation Sheet (Handout 4b_3, p. 93)

Estimated Time

90 minutes in class and, possibly, some additional time outside of class

LESSON PLAN

Introduce the Lesson

Ask the students the following introductory questions to determine what they know and what they think about those who run for office; the factors that have an impact on the electoral system; and the behavior of voters. Write their responses on the board.

> ➤ Why do people run for elected office?
> ➤ Who runs for office?
> ➤ What are the most important factors in determining the outcome of an election?
> ➤ Who votes?
> ➤ Why do people vote the way they do?

Explain that the panelists on Program 4 will answer these questions and others regarding the electoral system in the United States.

Give each student a copy of Terms to Know (Handout 4b_1, p. 91) and review each term to ensure that they have a clear understanding of what each term means.

View the Program

> ➤ Give each student a copy of the Viewing Questions (Handout 4b_2, p. 92).
> ➤ Ask the students to answer each of the questions using the information presented by the panelists.
> ➤ After showing the program, ask for volunteers to answer the Viewing Questions.
> ➤ Compare these answers with the responses students gave to the introductory questions.
> ➤ Point out significant differences between the two sets of answers.

Critical Thinking Exercise

The lack of participation by young people in the electoral process continues to be seen as a sign of weakness in the U.S. electoral system. Ask the students, working either individually or in pairs, to develop a strategy aimed at reversing this trend. The strategy should include the following components:

➤ a description of the problem

➤ a proposed solution to the problem

➤ a plan for implementing the proposed solution

➤ an evaluation that includes

  • the practicality of the solution and implementation plan

  • an analysis of the constitutionality of the solution

To assist students in determining if the solution is constitutional, remind them of the following limitations that the U.S. Constitution and state constitutions place upon governments:

➤ Government is not allowed to interfere with a person's freedom of belief.

➤ Government is not allowed to place unreasonable and unfair limits on a person's freedom of expression.

➤ Government is not allowed to invade a person's privacy without just cause.

➤ Government is not allowed to make laws that unreasonably or unfairly discriminate against people on the basis of race, religion, age, ethnic group, or gender.

LESSON PLAN

Conclude the Lesson

Give each student a copy of the Strategy Evaluation Sheet (Handout 4b_3. p. 93). Explain that each student or pair of students will present a strategy, and the class members will evaluate each strategy using the criteria on the evaluation sheet. When the presentations have been completed, ask the students to select the strategy they believe is the strongest, based on the evaluations.

Conclude the lesson by asking the students this overarching question:

➤ How well does the electoral process work?

Supplemental / Additional Activities

1 Have the class pursue the implementation of the strategy they judged to be the strongest.

2 Ask the students to research a member of Congress. They should include the following information in their reports: biographical data, record of public service, position on a current issue, future aspirations, and current job approval rating by the member's constituents.

3 Ask the students to take and defend a position on one of the following statements:

➤ Democracy is strengthened when a legislature is primarily composed of citizen legislators.

➤ Partisanship is weakening representative democracy in the United States.

➤ Gerrymandering has made elections moot in the United States.

➤ Redistricting should be taken out of the hands of legislative bodies.

4 Ask the students to compose an essay explaining low voter turnout for elections in the United States.

5 Ask the students to identify five members of Congress whom they would classify as citizen legislators and five whom they would classify as professional legislators. The students should explain their reasons for classifying each member as they did.

Terms to Know

➤ amateur legislator

➤ bipartisan

➤ citizen legislator

➤ electorate

➤ gerrymandering

➤ incumbent

➤ independent

➤ nonpartisan

➤ partisan

➤ party affiliation

➤ professional legislator

➤ redistricting

Viewing Questions

1 What are the two views of representation?

2 Why do people run for office?

3 Who runs for office?

4 What are some of the barriers for candidates who want to run for public office?

5 Why do people vote?

6 Why do they vote the way they do?

7 What are some reasons people do not vote?

**Strategy
Evaluation
Sheet**

Directions

For each criterion, score the strategy on a scale of 1–5, with 5 being the best score. Add the scores for each criterion to determine the total score for the strategy.

SCORE

1 poor

2 fair

3 average

4 above average

5 excellent

▼

Description of the problem
- ➤ accurate
- ➤ clearly stated
- ➤ thorough
- ➤ enhances understanding

Proposed solution
- ➤ easy to understand
- ➤ well-reasoned
- ➤ appropriate
- ➤ realistic

Plan for implementation
- ➤ well-organized
- ➤ adequate
- ➤ practical
- ➤ has potential for success

Evaluation
- ➤ describes the advantages and disadvantages
- ➤ persuasive
- ➤ adequately defends constitutionality of strategy

NOTES

Total   **Scorer's Name**

How Do Representatives Work to Represent Us?

Program 5 Overview

A panel of three congressional scholars describes how the 535 members of the U.S. Congress represent a diverse population of more than 280 million citizens. Through the course of their discussion, the panelists address such topics as who the members of Congress are and what they are trying to do; the role of interest groups; representatives' responsiveness to constituencies; the role of legislative staff; the subtleties of lawmaking; the characteristics of a model representative; representation by delegates and trustees; representation of voters who favor a losing candidate; and the strengths and weaknesses inherent in the legislative process. The program concludes with a description of the essential elements of the democratic process and the importance of citizens understanding these elements.

Objectives	By the end of this lesson students should be able to
	➤ define each of the Terms to Know
	➤ distinguish between the delegate and trustee models of representation
	➤ describe at least two strengths and two weaknesses of the legislative process
	➤ explain the role of congressional staffers in the legislative process
	➤ examine the role of interest groups in the legislative process
	➤ recommend and prioritize five characteristics of a good representative

Terms to Know

collective	lobbyist
constituents	partisan
deliberate	public interest
entrepreneur	public policy
The Federalist	representative as delegate
legislative staff	representative as trustee
legislator	special interest group
lexicon	

Materials Needed

➤ Program 5: How Do Representatives Work to Represent Us?

➤ One copy per student of Which Responsibilities Should the Representative Fulfill? (Handout 5a_1, pp. 100–102)

➤ One copy per group of Representative Martin's Chart of Considerations (Handout 5a_2, p. 103)

➤ Debate Topics (p. 104)

Estimated Time

90 minutes of class time

LESSON PLAN

Introduce the Lesson

To begin the lesson, ask the students to form either a diad or triad then read Which Responsibilities Should the Representative Fulfill? (Handout 5a_1, pp. 100–102).

Assign each diad or triad a persona from the following groups: Democratic Club, Association of Aged and Retired Persons, Retired Army Officers, Bankers Association, Residents Near the Base, and Supporters of Reducing Defense Spending.

The students should read the scenario then fill in the chart provided, based on their assigned persona.

The diad or triad should share its answers to the questions on the handout Representative Martin's Chart of Considerations (Handout 5a_2, p. 103), focusing on the last question:

➤ What should Representative Martin do?

Transitional Point

Ask the class the following questions:

➤ What problems did Representative Martin face?
➤ How might she try to resolve the dilemma?

View the Program

The students should view the program keeping Representative Martin's dilemma in mind.

Critical Thinking Exercise

After viewing the program, ask the students to identify at least five important concepts from the program and to describe how they might relate to Representative Martin's dilemma.

Transitional Point	Divide the class into groups of five or six and assign each group one of the Debate Topics (p. 104). Each group should then be subdivided into two smaller groups. Each of these smaller groups will be assigned either the positive or negative side of its group's topic and will develop a defense of that position.
Conclude the Lesson	The two smaller groups will come together and share their positions. This larger group will present both sides of its topic to the rest of the class.
Homework	Have the students complete one of the following exercises:

➤ Ask the students to select a debate topic, take a position on the subject, and write an essay defending that position.

➤ Ask the students to reconsider the dilemma of Representative Martin. Have them write an essay recommending a course of action for her and defending the reasons for their recommendation.

Supplemental / Additional Activities

1 Assign the class to read *The Federalist No.10*. Have them summarize and discuss the arguments put forth. Ask the students if these ideas and sentiments still ring true today.

2 Choose a public policy issue within the local community and then research what the local representative (e.g., council member, assemblyperson, etc.) has done with regard to that issue during his or her tenure.

3 Invite a congressional staffer from the local office to speak to the class about his or her role in the congressional office.

HANDOUT 5a_1

Taking and Defending a Position

Which Responsibilities Should the Representative Fulfill?*

Working with your partner(s), read the following situation and complete the task found at the end. Be prepared to share your work with the class.

Representative Martin's dilemma:

➤ Should the air force base be closed?

Times had changed. The Soviet Union had collapsed. The Cold War was over. The United States could reduce the size and cost of the military. Taxes could be decreased, and money could be spent on other programs.

The military's Base Closure Committee had submitted a list of military bases around the country that were not needed anymore. The president had approved the list and sent it to Congress. Now it was time for Congress to act.

As Representative Martin listened to the debate among other members of the House of Representatives, she was troubled. She knew she was expected to express her opinion and cast her vote on the base closure bill being discussed, but she was faced with competing and even conflicting responsibilities and interests.

The bill, if made into law, would eliminate an air force base in the district of another member of Congress in her state, a fellow Democrat. In addition, the air force base was located in the second largest city in the state and provided more jobs than any other employer in the city. If the base were to be closed, thousands of people would be put out of work, and the city's economy might be devastated.

Although the air force base was not in her district, Martin had originally opposed the idea of closing it. She had not felt strongly about the issue, nor had her

*Adapted from *Foundations of Democracy,* Middle School Level, "Responsibility," Lesson 9, pp. 147–149. © 1993, 2005 Center for Civic Education.

constituents, who lived in a distant part of the state. Her opposition to the bill was partially due to her friendship with the Democratic representative from that area, who had made it his top priority to keep the base open. It was also the result of her belief that if she were to support her colleague on this issue, her favor would be returned on other matters.

The issue was receiving a great deal of attention. Representative Martin and other members of Congress were feeling pressure from various groups interested in the outcome. For example, just the week before, she had met with members of the Democratic Club from her community who had come to discuss various local matters. The group had provided considerable assistance in her election and, she hoped, would do the same in the next election. In the course of the conversation, the group made it clear that they were in favor of keeping the base open, and they expected her to continue to support her fellow Democrat.

As luck would have it, as soon as this group left Representative Martin's office, a representative of the Association of Aged and Retired Persons entered. He tried to persuade her to vote in favor of the bill so that taxes could be reduced. Martin had received substantial campaign contributions from members of the Association, and many of her constituents were retired and lived on fixed incomes.

Representative Martin also received visits from

➤ a group of retired army officers, who insisted that she had an obligation to support the bill because it would make the military more efficient

➤ the Banker's Association from her district, which took the position that by opposing the bill she would be helping the economy of the state

➤ people who lived near the air force base and opposed its closure

➤ people who favored the reduction of defense spending and supported the bill

She listened to all of them with equal attention.

Faced with these conflicting demands, Representative Martin reflected on her responsibilities. She was responsible not only to her constituents, her supporters, and the other members of her party, but also to the interests of all the people in the state and, for that matter, the nation. There was no doubt that the potential savings from closing military bases around the country were enormous and would help the government balance the budget. At the same time, it was clear that closing the air force base would seriously hurt the economy of the second largest city in the state. Taking these and other considerations into account, she, as a member of Congress, was responsible for making the best decision possible. She could not please everyone or fulfill what she saw as conflicting responsibilities to her various constituents, colleagues, and interests.

Developing and Presenting Group Positions

You and your partners have been assigned to take on the persona of one of these groups:

- ➤ Democratic Club
- ➤ Association of Aged and Retired Persons
- ➤ Retired Army Officers
- ➤ Bankers Association
- ➤ Residents Near the Base
- ➤ Supporters of Reducing Defense Spending

As a member of your group, suggest what Representative Martin should do and why. Fill out Representative Martin's Chart of Considerations (Handout 5a_2, p. 103), which is provided to help you justify a position among Representative Martin's competing responsibilities. Once you have completed the task, share your group's views and position with the rest of the class.

Representative Martin's Chart of Considerations*

➤ Name of Group

1   What responsibility does the group you represent wish Representative Martin to fulfill?

2   What might be the *rewards* for fulfilling the responsibility?

3   What might be the *penalties* for not fulfilling the responsibility?

4   What is the *source* of the responsibility?

5   What would be the *benefits* of fulfilling the responsibility?

6   What would be the *costs* of fulfilling the responsibility?

7   How *important* is fulfilling this responsibility?

8   What other interests and values are related to fulfilling this responsibility?

9   Is there an alternative or a compromise solution?

10   What should Representative Martin do? Why?

*Adapted from *Foundations of Democracy*, Middle School Level, "Responsibility," Lesson 9, p. 150. © 1993, 2005 Center for Civic Education.

DEBATE TOPICS

1   Special interest groups:
    voicing the needs of constituents
    or attempts to secure selfish goals?

2   Which model of representation works best:
    delegate or trustee?

3   Congressional staff:
    legislative necessity or
    unaccountable exercise of power?

4   The lawmaking process:
    careful, thoughtful, and deliberate
    or sluggish, partisan, and stalemated?

5   Special interest groups:
    promoting the general welfare
    or divisive factions?

Objectives

By the end of this lesson students should be able to

➤ define each of the Terms to Know

➤ demonstrate an understanding of
  - those who serve as members of Congress
  - the role of legislative staff in the lawmaking process
  - the strengths and weaknesses of the legislative process
  - the methods used to represent constituents

➤ take and defend a position on what
  makes a model representative

Terms to Know

compromise	majority party
constituent	minority party
delegate model	proactive
deliberation	public interest
legislative committee	public policy
legislative staff	special interest group
legislator	trustee model
lobbyist	

Materials Needed

➤ Program 5: How Do Representatives
  Work to Represent Us?

➤ One copy per student of Terms
  to Know (Handout 5b_1, p. 109)

➤ One copy per student of Viewing
  Questions (Handout 5b_2, p. 110)

➤ One copy per student of The Model
  Representative (Handout 5b_3, p. 111)

Estimated Time

60 minutes in class and one
to two hours outside of class

LESSON PLAN

Introduce the Lesson

To get a sense of what the students know about Congress and the way it functions, ask the following questions:

➤ Can you identify any member of Congress and can you give any information about that person? How have you come to know this information?

➤ How many members of Congress are there? How many of those serve in the House of Representatives and how many serve in the Senate?

➤ How many senators and representatives are there in Congress from our state?

➤ How can the members of Congress adequately represent all the people in the United States?

➤ How can our senators and representatives adequately represent all the people in our state?

➤ How do you think the members of Congress are doing in representing the interests of the American people?

➤ How do you think our congressional delegation is doing in representing the interests of the people in our state?

Explain that the panelists in Program 5 will address some of these questions and others as they talk about how members of Congress work.

Give each student a copy of the Terms to Know (Handout 5b_1, p. 109). Ask the students to listen for these terms as they watch the program. Check to see how many of the terms the students already know and understand. Review these terms after viewing the program.

View the Program

➤ Give each student a copy of the Viewing Questions (Handout 5b_2, p. 110).
➤ Ask the students to answer each question using the information presented in the program.
➤ After viewing the program, ask for volunteers to share their responses to the Viewing Questions. Clarify any points that need to be understood more thoroughly.

Critical Thinking Exercise

The population of congressional districts continues to grow, as does the diversity of interests in America. How then can Congress, whose size remains fixed at 535, adequately represent the public interest? How does our government continue to be a representative democracy?

The purpose of this three-part exercise is to allow students the opportunity to weigh in on these questions. Begin by distributing a copy of The Model Representative (Handout 5b_3, p. 111) to each student. (The handout has student instructions similar to those below.)

PART ONE

Guidelines for members of Congress

Ask the students, either individually or in pairs, to develop a set of guidelines that they believe representatives should follow to ensure fair representation of their constituents. These guidelines should include, but not be limited to, the following elements:

- ➤ ways to identify the interests of constituents
- ➤ effective use of legislative staff
- ➤ how information provided by interest groups may be used
- ➤ how information provided by lobbyists may be used
- ➤ how much reliance to place on one's own knowledge, judgment, and beliefs
- ➤ extent to which one should make decisions that reflect the views of one's constituents
- ➤ extent to which one should act on behalf of the common good
- ➤ degree to which one should compromise

PART TWO

Why should members of Congress follow these guidelines?

Ask the students to compose an essay explaining why their guidelines, if followed, will help to ensure that elected representatives fairly represent the public interest.

PART THREE

Possible solutions to representing a diversity of interests

Ask the students to identify at least two possible solutions to the ever-present problem of ensuring that, collectively, our representatives in Congress can and shall represent the diversity of interests that exist in the United States.

LESSON PLAN

Conclude the Lesson

Ask the students to share with the class their best guidelines for members of Congress. Allow other students to comment on these guidelines. Conclude the discussion with students giving their solutions to the problem of how Congress can and should represent the diversity of interests in the United States.

Supplemental / Additional Activities

1 Ask the students to develop a biographical sketch of a legislator and include information that shows how this person attempts to represent his or her constituents.

2 Ask the students to write an essay titled "If I Were a Member of Congress." In the essay students should describe how they would work to fairly represent their constituents.

3 Ask the students to write an essay describing the model representative.

4 Divide the class into two groups for a debate of the statement:

   ➤ Lobbyists are a vital part of the legislative process in a representative democracy.

   One group must take and defend the affirmative position; the other group must take and defend the negative position.

   Allow each side to present their position, then allow students from each side to cross-examine the other side. Conclude the debate by allowing yet other students from each side to present the closing statements.

5 Ask the students to take and defend a position on one the following statements:

   ➤ Legislative representatives have a duty to represent all their constituents, not just the majority.

   ➤ The partisanship found in legislative bodies today means that these entities no longer represent the public interest; rather, they represent the majority interest.

Terms to Know

➤ compromise

➤ constituent

➤ delegate model

➤ deliberation

➤ legislative committee

➤ legislative staff

➤ legislator

➤ lobbyist

➤ majority party

➤ minority party

➤ proactive

➤ public interest

➤ public policy

➤ special interest group

➤ trustee model

HANDOUT 5b_2

Viewing Questions

1   According to James Madison in *The Federalist*, how might Congress can determine what is in the public interest?

_____

_____

2   What are special interest groups?

_____

_____

3   What are some ways young people can influence their representatives?

_____

_____

4   What is the role of the legislative staff?

_____

_____

5   What is the role of the committee in the legislative process?

_____

_____

6   What are some of the strengths of a legislative body versus an executive?

_____

_____

7   What are some characteristics of a model legislator?

_____

_____

8   What are some of the strengths and weaknesses of the legislative process?

_____

_____

The Model Representative

PART ONE

Guidelines for members of Congress

Develop a set of guidelines that you believe representatives should follow to ensure fair representation of their constituents. These guidelines should include, but not be limited to, the following elements:

➤ ways to identify the interests of constituents

➤ effective use of legislative staff

➤ how information provided by interest groups may be used

➤ how information provided by lobbyists may be used

➤ how much reliance to place on one's own knowledge, judgment, and beliefs

➤ extent to which one should make decisions that reflect the views of one's constituents

➤ extent to which one should act on behalf of the common good

➤ degree to which one should compromise

PART TWO

Why should members of Congress follow these guidelines?

Compose an essay explaining why your guidelines, if followed, will help to ensure that elected representatives fairly represent the public interest.

PART THREE

Possible solutions to representing a diversity of interests

Identify at least two possible solutions to the ever-present problem of ensuring that, collectively, our representatives in Congress can and shall represent the diversity of interests that exists in the United States.

What Are Citizens' Roles in Representative Democracy?

Program 6 Overview

Three congressional scholars explore the roles citizens must play in a representative democracy for the system to work. Among the topics discussed are citizen engagement, becoming an informed voter, and the accountability of elected officials. The panelists point out the importance of frequent elections in keeping members of Congress responsive to their constituencies. They also discuss the fact that the United States is almost evenly divided politically and examine the impact this has on the functioning of Congress as it attempts to represent the people. The program concludes with a brief look at two alternatives to our current system of representative democracy.

Objectives

By the end of this lesson students should be able to

➤ define each of the Terms to Know

➤ identify two positive and two negative influences of lobbying groups on political campaigns

➤ describe the role of the media in political campaigns

➤ describe the effectiveness of representatives at fulfilling their campaign promises

➤ propose two ways in which young people can be motivated to participate in a democratic society

➤ discuss the role of the citizen in a representative democracy

Terms to Know

accountability
benign dictator
consensus
constituency
direct democracy

gridlock
institutional responsibility
partisan
representative democracy
republic

Materials Needed

➤ Program 6: What Are Citizens' Roles in Representative Democracy?

➤ Teacher Information Sheet — What Is Responsibility? (p. 118)

➤ How Can Citizens Participate? activity sheet (Handout 6a_1, pp. 119–120)

Estimated Time

50 minutes of class time

LESSON PLAN

Introduce the Lesson

Begin the lesson by asking the students to take a couple of minutes to answer the following questions:

➤ What is responsibility?

➤ What are three examples of responsibilities you have?

Place students' definitions on the board and list some examples.

Transitional Point

Ask the class, "Where do responsibilities come from?" (sources of responsibilities).

List as many answers as they can come up with, then complete the list for them. (Use the What Is Responsibility? Teacher Information Sheet on p. 118 to help you.)

Have the students categorize their responsibilities under the source from which they originate. If some sources don't have examples, ask students to suggest one or two for each.

Transitional Point

Tell the students that for the rest of the lesson they will concentrate on the following topic:

➤ Civic Responsibilities and Citizens' Roles in Representative Democracy.

View the Program

➤ Prior to viewing the program, ask the students to list civic responsibilities and to identify ways we can participate in our representative democracy.

➤ Write their answers on the board but do not complete the list for them.

➤ Have the list visible while the students watch the program.

➤ After viewing the program, ask the students to see if they can add responsibilities to the list on the board.

Critical Thinking Exercise

Divide the class into small groups and ask them to complete the exercise on the How Can Citizens Participate? activity sheet (Handout 6a_1, pp. 119–120).

Conclude the Lesson

Ask groups to share their responses.

Supplemental / Additional Activities

1 Have the students write letters to the Athenian statesman Pericles, explaining why they agree or disagree with his statement:

➤ "We… do not call a man who takes no part in public life quiet or unambitious; we call such a man useless."

2 Have the students select several rights we enjoy as American citizens. For each right listed, have them indicate one or more corresponding responsibility.

What is Responsibility?*

Responsibility is a duty or obligation to do something or not to do something.

SOURCES OF RESPONSIBILITY

➤ **Promises**
When one individual makes a promise to another, that individual takes on the responsibility or obligation of keeping the promise or "living up to his or her word." Sometimes people make promises in the form of legal agreements called contracts. At other times, promises are informal. You should recognize that when you make a promise, you consent or agree to fulfill a responsibility or obligation.

➤ **Assignments**
Sometimes people assign or impose responsibilities on others.

➤ **Appointments**
In some situations, people may be chosen for or appointed to positions that carry responsibilities.

➤ **Occupations**
Each occupation or job carries certain responsibilities.

➤ **Laws**
Laws place responsibilities on almost everyone in society.

➤ **Customs**
Some responsibilities come from customs—traditions or standard practices developed over time—that people in society are expected to follow.

➤ **Citizenship**
In our country, people have certain responsibilities just because they are citizens.

➤ **Moral principles**
Moral principles are rules or standards of conduct based on principles of right and wrong.

*Adapted from *Foundations of Democracy*, High School Level; "Responsibility," Lessons 1, 2, pp. 113–120. © 1993, 2005 Center for Civic Education.

How Can Citizens Participate*

Almost all citizens have the right to participate in governing our nation. They may choose among many different ways of doing this. Some ways to participate are listed below.

EXAMINING PARTICIPATION

Your class has been divided into small groups. Each group will read the list of ways in which citizens can participate, then answer the questions on the next page. Your group will be asked to share its answers with other groups in the class.

WAYS CITIZENS CAN PARTICIPATE

➤ looking for information in newspapers, magazines, and reference materials, and judging its accuracy

➤ voting in local, state, and national elections

➤ participating in a political discussion

➤ signing a petition

➤ trying to persuade someone to vote a certain way

➤ wearing a button or displaying a bumper sticker

➤ writing letters to elected representatives

➤ contributing money to a party or candidate

➤ attending meetings to gain information, discuss issues, or lend support

➤ campaigning for a candidate

➤ lobbying for laws that are of special interest

➤ taking part in marches, boycotts, sit-ins, or other forms of protest

➤ serving as a juror

➤ running for office

➤ holding public office

➤ serving the country through military or other service

➤ disobeying laws and taking the consequences to demonstrate that a law or policy is unjust

(Continued on next page)

*Adapted from *We the People: The Citizen and the Constitution*, Middle School Level; Lesson 28, pp. 123–125. © 1988 Center for Civic Education.

QUESTIONS

1 What are the advantages and disadvantages
   of each form of participation listed?

2 Are all these forms of participation equally important
   in protecting our basic rights? Why or why not?
   If not, which seem the most important?

3 Which of these forms of participation
   are the most effective? Explain why.

4 Are there other things that young people
   can do that are not on this list? Name them.

Objectives	By the end of this lesson students should be able to
	➤ define each of the Terms to Know
	➤ demonstrate an understanding of the citizen's roles in a representative democracy
	➤ demonstrate an understanding of the importance of an informed and engaged citizenry in representative democracy

Terms to Know

absentee ballot	gridlock
benign dictator	institutional responsibility
campaign	middle ground
congressional oversight	partisan
consensus	prerogatives
constituency	representative democracy
direct democracy	republican form of government
"fifty-fifty" nation	

Materials Needed

➤ Program 6: What Are Citizens' Roles in Representative Democracy?

➤ One copy per student of Terms to Know (Handout 6b_1, p. 126)

➤ One copy per student of Viewing Questions (Handout 6b_2, p. 127)

➤ One copy per student of My Representative's Report Card, (Handout 6b_4, p. 129) and the Example (Handout 6b_3, p. 128)

Estimated Time

90 minutes in class and one to two hours outside of class

LESSON PLAN

Introduce the Lesson

Before viewing the program ask the students the following questions:

- ➤ What is the citizen's role in a representative democracy?
- ➤ How important is voting in maintaining representative democracy?
- ➤ How can citizens inform themselves about the issues that are important to them?
- ➤ How can citizens inform themselves about what their representatives are doing?
- ➤ Are campaigns essential for representative government?
- ➤ Who is most likely to vote in any given election?
- ➤ How can citizens avoid being misled by those with a particular bias about candidates seeking office?

View the Program

Explain that the panelists will address these and other questions as they discuss the roles of citizens in a representative democracy.

Give each student a copy of the Terms to Know (Handout 6b_1, p. 126). Review these terms before viewing the program to see how many of them are understood. Ask the students to listen for the terms as they watch the program. Tell the students you will review the terms later.

- ➤ Give each student a copy of the Viewing Questions (Handout 6b_2, p. 127).
- ➤ Ask the students to answer each question using the information presented in the program.
- ➤ After showing the program, ask for volunteers to share their responses to the Viewing Questions. Clarify any points that need to be understood more thoroughly.
- ➤ Check to see if all students now understand each of the Terms to Know.

Critical Thinking Exercise

Explain that the students are going to develop a report card/rubric and will use it to determine how well one of their elected representatives represents his or her constituency.

➤ Divide the class into five groups (four in Nebraska) of equal size.

➤ Ask the students in each group to identify three to five public policy issues that are important to them and/or other citizens in their community or state. One student in each group should record the issues.

➤ When the students have finished identifying the issues, ask each group to post its list for the entire class to see.

➤ Review the lists and determine whether each issue is within the purview of the national government, state government, or both.

- If a group's list consists mainly of federal issues, assign one of your U.S. senators or your U.S. representative to that group. If there are fewer than three federal issues on the list, ask the group to replace a state issue with a third federal issue.

- If a group's list consists mainly of state issues, assign your state senator or state representative/assembly person to that group. If there are fewer than three state issues on the list, ask the group to replace a federal issue with a state issue.

- If a group's list consists of an equal number of federal and state issues, ask the group to replace either the state issues with federal issues or vice versa. Then assign the group the appropriate elected official to research.

- If a group's list consists of issues that are within the purview of both the national and state government, assign the group one of your members of Congress or a state legislator.

(continued on next page)

LESSON PLAN

Critical Thinking Exercise
(continued)

➤ Give each student a copy of My Representative's Report Card (Handout 6b_4, p. 129) and the Example (Handout 6b_3, p. 128). Explain that the assignment requires the students to complete these three steps:

1 Determine the position that the elected official assigned to their group has taken on each of the issues they have identified. To complete this step, students should

- enter the issues in the first column

- choose three indices they believe will give them the clearest indication of the representative's position on the issues

- enter the indices in the top row of columns two, three, and four of the chart, as shown in the Example

2 Determine, to the best of their ability, the position of the official's constituents on the issues. For example, students might learn, through the results of a published report, that most people are in favor of a particular government action on an issue. This information should be entered in the last column of the chart.

3 Compose an essay that summarizes their findings and answers the following question:

- To what extent does my elected representative represent the views of his or her constituency?

Conclude the Lesson

Have one student from each group share only the summaries of his or her findings with the class. Ask the class to indicate how well they think the representative represents his or her constituency. Conclude the lesson by asking the students this overarching question:

➤ What can you and other constituents do to ensure that elected officials provide adequate representation?

Supplemental / Additional Activities

1 Ask the students to read *The Federalist No. 57* and identify the five arguments James Madison makes to support his position that the members of the House of Representatives will truly represent the many and not the few. Then each student should choose the argument that he or she believes to be the most compelling and explain in an essay why it is the strongest.

2 Ask the students to take and defend a position on one of the following statements:

➤ Campaigns are a way of conveying information about a candidate to citizens that they would not otherwise get.

➤ Successful candidates keep a large percentage of the promises made while running for office.

➤ A "fifty-fifty" nation means that it is more difficult for representatives to truly represent their constituents.

➤ Low voter turnout weakens representative democracy.

3 Ask the students to develop a comprehensive list of the ways in which citizens who are too young to vote can make their positions on issues known and have those positions taken into account.

Terms to Know

➤ absentee ballot

➤ benign dictator

➤ campaign

➤ congressional oversight

➤ consensus

➤ constituency

➤ direct democracy

➤ "fifty-fifty" nation

➤ gridlock

➤ institutional responsibility

➤ middle ground

➤ partisan

➤ prerogatives

➤ representative democracy

➤ republican form of government

Viewing Questions

1 What are some of the citizens'
   roles in representative democracy?

2 In what ways are campaigns and elections
   essential to maintaining representative democracy?

3 What are some of the ways citizens
   can inform themselves about issues?

4 What are some of the ways citizens can keep
   track of what their representatives are doing?

5 What is the connection between the
   United States being a "fifty-fifty" nation
   and frequent gridlock in Congress?

6 Why is voting essential to the proper
   functioning of representative democracy?

HANDOUT 6b_3

<table>
<tr><td rowspan="2">Example of
My Representative's
Report Card</td><td colspan="4">➤ Name of the Representative

Mary Lopez</td></tr>
<tr><td colspan="4">➤ Serves in

State House of Representatives – District #2</td></tr>
</table>

The Issues	Index #1 *sponsored a bill dealing with the issue*	Index #2 *voted for or against a bill dealing with the issue*	Index #3 *campaigned for or against the issue*	Constituents' Position
sales tax on food and drugs	*has not sponsored a bill dealing with the issue*	*voted against a bill to eliminate sales tax in 2005*	*campaigned for keeping sales tax*	*68% in favor of eliminating sales tax, according to a recent newspaper poll*

My Representative's Report Card

➤ Name of the Representative

➤ Serves in

The Issues	Index #1	Index #2	Index #3	Constituents' Position

Bibliography

BIBLIOGRAPHY

PROGRAM 1

What Are the Roots of Representative Democracy?

Center for Civic Education. *We the People: The Citizen & the Constitution*, Units 1 and 2. Calabasas, CA: Center for Civic Education, 1995.

Davidson, Roger H. and Walter J. Oleszek. *Congress and Its Members*, 10th ed., Chap. 2. Washington, DC: CQ Press, 2005.

Rosenthal *et al. Republic on Trial: The Case for Representative Democracy*. Washington, DC: CQ Press, 2003.

PROGRAM 2

What Are Federalism and the Separation of Powers?

Bernstein, Richard, with Kym S. Rice. *Are We to Be a Nation: The Making of the Constitution*. Cambridge, MA: Harvard University Press, 1987.

Bowen, Catherine Drinker. *Miracle at Philadelphia*. Boston: Little, Brown & Co., 1966.

Center for Civic Education. *We The People: The Citizen & the Constitution*, Unit 2. Calabasas, CA: Center for Civic Education, 1995.

Cummings, Milton C., Jr., and David Wise. *Democracy Under Pressure: An Introduction to the American Political System*, Chaps. 2–3. Belmont, CA: Thomson-Wadsworth, 2005.

Rakove, Jack N. *Original Meanings: Politics and Ideas in the Making of the Constitution*. New York: Vintage Books, 1997.

Rhodehamel, John. *The Great Experiment: George Washington and the American Republic*. New Haven: Yale University Press; San Marino, CA: The Huntington Library, 1998.

PROGRAM 3

What Are the Responsibilities of Representatives, Executives, and Justices?

Binkley, Wilfred E. *President and Congress*. New York: Vintage Books, 1962.

Bunch, Lonnie C., III, *et al. The American Presidency: A Glorious Burden*. Washington, DC: The Smithsonian Institution Press, 2000.

Cummings, Milton C., Jr., and David Wise. *Democracy Under Pressure: An Introduction to the American Political System*, Chaps. 12–13. Belmont, CA: Thomson-Wadsworth, 2005.

DiClerico, Robert E. *The American President*, 5th ed. Upper Saddle River, NJ: Prentice Hall, 2000.

Edwards, George C., III, and Stephen J. Wayne. *Presidential Leadership: Politics and Policy Making*, 7th ed. Belmont, CA: Wadsworth Publishing, 2005.

Fisher, Louis. *Presidential War Power*, 2nd ed. Lawrence, KS: University Press of Kansas, 2003.

———. *Congressional Abdication on War and Spending*. College Station, TX: Texas A&M University Press, 2000.

Gould, Lewis L. *The Modern American Presidency*. Lawrence, KS: University Press of Kansas, 2005.

Greenstein, Fred I. *The Presidential Difference: Leadership Style from FDR to Clinton*. Princeton: Princeton University Press, 2001.

Hargrove, Erwin C. *The President as Leader*. Lawrence, KS: University Press of Kansas, 2003.

Jones, Charles O. *The Presidency in a Separated System*, 2nd ed. Washington, DC: Brookings Institution Press, 2005.

———. *Separate but Equal Branches: Congress and the Presidency*, 2nd ed. New York: Chatham House, 1999.

Pfiffner, James P. *The Strategic Presidency: Hitting the Ground Running*, 2nd ed. Lawrence, KS: University Press of Kansas, 2003.

———. *The Character Factor: How We Judge America's Presidents*. College Station, TX: Texas A&M University Press, 2004.

Rae, Nicol C., and Colton C. Campbell. *Impeaching Clinton: Partisan Strife on Capitol Hill*. Lawrence, KS: University Press of Kansas, 2003.

Thurber, James A., ed. *Rivals for Power: Presidential–Executive Relations*, 3rd ed. Lanham, MD: Rowman & Littlefield, 2005.

PROGRAM 4

Who Are Our Representatives and How Do We Choose Them?

Canon, David T. *Race, Redistricting, and Representation*. Chicago: University of Chicago Press, 1999.

Corrado, Anthony, *et al. New Campaign Finance Reform: A Sourcebook*. Washington, DC: Brookings Institution Press, 2005.

Cummings, Milton C., Jr., and David Wise. *Democracy Under Pressure*, 10th ed., Chaps. 10–11. Belmont, CA: Thomson-Wadsworth, 2005.

Davidson, Roger H. and Walter J. Oleszek. *Congress and Its Members*, 10th ed., Chaps. 3–4. Washington, DC: CQ Press, 2006.

Ehrenhalt, Alan. *The United States of Ambition*. New York: Random House, 1991.

Herrnson, Paul. *Congressional Elections: Campaigning at Home and in Washington*, 4th ed. Washington, DC: CQ Press, 2004.

Hibbing, John R., and Elizabeth Theiss-Morse. *Stealth Democracy: Americans' Beliefs about How Government Should Work*. Cambridge: Cambridge University Press, 2002.

Jacobson, Gary C. *The Politics of Congressional Elections*, 6th ed. New York: Pearson-Longman, 2004.

Loomis, Burdett. *The New American Politician*. New York: Basic Books, 1988.

O'Connor, Karen, ed., *Women and Congress: Running, Winning, and Ruling*. New York: Haworth Press, 2002.

Ornstein, Norman, and Thomas Mann, eds. *The Permanent Campaign and Its Future*. Washington, DC: American Enterprise Institute / Brookings Institution, 2000.

Palast, Greg. *The Best Democracy Money Can Buy*, revised ed. New York: Penguin-Plume Books, 2004.

Price, David E. *The Congressional Experience: The View from the Hill*, 2nd ed. Boulder, CO: Westview Press, 2000.

Shafer, Byron E., ed. *The State of American Politics*. Lanham, MD: Rowman & Littlefield, 2002.

Swers, Michele L. *The Difference Women Make: The Policy Impact of Women in Congress*. Chicago: University of Chicago Press, 2002.

Thurber, James A., ed. *The Battle for Congress: Consultants, Candidates, and Voters*. Washington, DC: Brookings Institution Press, 2001.

PROGRAM 5

How Do Representatives Work to Represent Us?

Binder, Sarah A. *Stalemate: Causes and Consequences of Legislative Gridlock*. Washington, DC: Brookings Institution Press, 2003.

Davidson, Roger H., and Walter J. Oleszek. *Congress and Its Members*, 10th ed., Chaps. 6–8. Washington, DC: CQ Press, 2005.

Dolan, Julie, and Marni Ezra. *CQ's Legislative Simulation*. Washington, DC: CQ Press, 2001.

Hamilton, Lee H. *How Congress Works, and Why You Should Care*. Bloomington, IN: Indiana University Press, 2004.

Josephy, Alvin M., Jr. *The American Heritage History of the Congress of the United States*. New York: McGraw-Hill, 1975.

Oleszek, Walter J. *Congressional Procedures and the Policy Process*, 6th ed. Washington, DC: CQ Press, 2003.

Sinclair, Barbara. *Unorthodox Lawmaking: New Legislative Processes in the U.S. Congress*. Washington, DC: CQ Press, 2000.

PROGRAM 6

What Are Citizens' Roles in Representative Democracy?

Center for Civic Education and National Conference of State Legislatures. *We the People: Project Citizen*. Calabasas, CA: Center for Civic Education, 1996.

Crenson, Matthew A., and Benjamin Ginsberg. *Downsizing Democracy: How America Sidelined Its Citizens and Privatized Its Public*. Baltimore, MD: Johns Hopkins University Press, 2002.

Fiorina, Morris P., with Samuel J. Abrams and Jeremy C. Pope. *Culture War? The Myth of a Polarized America*, 2nd ed. New York: Pearson-Longman, 2006.

Green, Donald P., and Alan S. Gerber. *Get Out the Vote! How to Increase Voter Turnout*. Washington, DC: Brookings Institution Press, 2004.

Patterson, Thomas E. *The Vanishing Voter: Public Involvement in an Age of Uncertainty*. New York: Vintage Books, 2003.

Skocpol, Theda, and Morris P. Fiorina, eds. *Civic Engagement in American Democracy*. Washington, DC: Brookings Institution Press; New York: Russell Sage Foundation, 1999.

Wattenberg, Martin P. *Where Have All the Voters Gone?* Cambridge, MA: Harvard University Press, 2002.

Correlations

Major concepts, events, and people found in each program of the video series are correlated to corresponding lessons in the Level III *We the People: The Citizen & the Constitution* text.

Program 1_ What Are the Roots of Representative Democracy?

We the People: The Citizen & the Constitution

CONCEPT ▼	▼ 1 — 1–9 — What Are the Philosophical and Historical Foundations of the American Political System?	▼ 2 — 10–17 — How Did the Framers Create the Constitution?	▼ 3 — 18–22 — How Did the Values and Principles Embodied in the Constitution Shape American Institutions and Practices?	▼ 4 — 23–28 — How Have the Protections of the Bill of Rights Been Developed and Expanded?	▼ 5 — 29–34 — What Rights Does the Bill of Rights Protect?	▼ 6 — 35–40 — What Are the Roles of the Citizen in American Democracy?
American Revolution	LESSON 8					
aristocracy	LESSON 3					
Aristotle	LESSON 2–3					
Articles of Confederation		LESSON 10				
Articles of the U.S. Constitution		LESSON 13–14				
Athenian Greece	LESSON 2					
bicameral legislature		LESSON 12				
Bill of Rights	LESSON 6, 9		LESSON 18–19			
branches of government		LESSON 12–14				
checks and balances	LESSON 2					
civic virtue	LESSON 3–4	LESSON 16–17				LESSON 35
Civil Rights Movement				LESSON 26		
Civil War				LESSON 23		
colonial governments	LESSON 7					
common good	LESSON 3–4	LESSON 16–17				LESSON 35–36
consent of the governed	LESSON 1–2, 6–8					
covenant	LESSON 7					
Declaration of Independence	LESSON 1–2, 8					
democracy	LESSON 2–3					
direct democracy	LESSON 2					
equality	LESSON 7			LESSON 25–28		

CONCEPT ▸	▸ 1	▸ 2	▸ 3	▸ 4	▸ 5	▸ 6
executive branch		LESSON 12, 14	LESSON 18–19	LESSON 24–25		
expanding right to vote	LESSON 1, 4			LESSON 27		
individual worth	LESSON 6–7, 9	LESSON 12–13, 15, 17				
issues of representation	LESSON 1–2, 8					
John Locke	LESSON 1–2, 8					
judicial branch		LESSON 12, 14	LESSON 18–19, 21			
large territory as republic		LESSON 16				
legislative branch	LESSON 2, 5, 7, 9	LESSON 12–13, 17		LESSON 25	LESSON 34	
limited government	LESSON 5–6	LESSON 13–14, 16–17	LESSON 18–19			
Magna Carta	LESSON 5–6				LESSON 31–32	
Mayflower Compact	LESSON 7					
Montesquieu	LESSON 3, 6				LESSON 34	
natural rights	LESSON 1–4, 7–9					
need for a stronger central government		LESSON 10–11				
parliament	LESSON 6, 8					LESSON 38
Philadelphia Convention		LESSON 11				
popular sovereignty	LESSON 9					
Preamble	Intro, PAGE ix					
public good	LESSON 3					LESSON 36
ratification of U.S. Constitution		LESSON 16–17				
the Reformation	LESSON 4					
the Renaissance	LESSON 4					
representative democracy	LESSON 3	LESSON 16–17				
republic	LESSON 2–3	LESSON 16–17				
right to revolution	LESSON 2, 8					
rule of law	LESSON 5–7				LESSON 32	
self-government	LESSON 7–9					
separated and balanced powers	LESSON 2–3, 7–9					
slavery	LESSON 7	LESSON 13				
state differences			LESSON 22			
state legislatures	LESSON 9			LESSON 23		

Program 2_ What Are Federalism and the Separation of Powers?

We the People: The Citizen & the Constitution

CONCEPT	UNIT ▸ 1 — LESSON 1–9 — What Are the Philosophical and Historical Foundations of the American Political System?	▸ 2 — 10–17 — How Did the Framers Create the Constitution?	▸ 3 — 18–22 — How Did the Values and Principles Embodied in the Constitution Shape American Institutions and Practices?	▸ 4 — 23–28 — How Have the Protections of the Bill of Rights Been Developed and Expanded?	▸ 5 — 29–34 — What Rights Does the Bill of Rights Protect?	▸ 6 — 35–40 — What Are the Roles of the Citizen in American Democracy?
advantages/disadvantages of federalism			LESSON 22			
Articles of Confederation		LESSON 10				
checks and balances		LESSON 13–14				
Civil War	LESSON 2					
compromise		LESSON 13				
confederation		LESSON 10	LESSON 22			
enumerated powers		LESSON 13, 17				
executive branch		LESSON 12, 14	LESSON 18–19	LESSON 24–25		
federal funding			LESSON 22			
federalism			LESSON 22			
federal powers			LESSON 22			
House of Representatives		LESSON 12–14, 16	LESSON 19			
judicial branch		LESSON 12, 14	LESSON 18–19, 21	LESSON 23		
judicial review		LESSON 14	LESSON 21			
legislative branch	LESSON 2, 6–9	LESSON 12–14, 17	LESSON 18, 22	LESSON 24–26		
limitations of power					LESSON 33–34	
Miranda rights					LESSON 34	
Philadelphia Convention		LESSON 11–17				
power of the purse		LESSON 13				
powers of Congress		LESSON 13				
powers of the president		LESSON 14				

CONCEPT ▶	▶ 1	▶ 2	▶ 3	▶ 4	▶ 5	▶ 6
reserved powers			LESSON 19			
responsibilities of citizens						LESSON 35–36
roles of Congress		LESSON 13–17	LESSON 22			
Senate		LESSON 12–14	LESSON 18–19			
separation of powers	LESSON 2, 6–9	LESSON 12–14, 17	LESSON 18, 22	LESSON 24–26		
Shays' Rebellion		LESSON 10				
state powers			LESSON 22			
veto/veto override		LESSON 14				
Washington's presidency			LESSON 18			
weaknesses of confederation		LESSON 10				

Program 3_ What Are the Roles of Representatives, Executives, and Justices in Our Democracy?

We the People: The Citizen & the Constitution	1	2	3	4	5	6
UNIT ▸						
LESSON ▸	1–9	10–17	18–22	23–28	29–34	35–40
TITLE ▸	What Are the Philosophical and Historical Foundations of the American Political System?	How Did the Framers Create the Constitution?	How Did the Values and Principles Embodied in the Constitution Shape American Institutions and Practices?	How Have the Protections of the Bill of Rights Been Developed and Expanded?	What Rights Does the Bill of Rights Protect?	What Are the Roles of the Citizen in American Democracy?
CONCEPT ▸						
checks and balances	LESSON 2, 6–7, 9	LESSON 12–17	LESSON 18–19, 21	LESSON 23–28	LESSON 29–34	
Congress and the presidency	LESSON 2	LESSON 13–14				
electoral college		LESSON 14				
executive branch		LESSON 12, 14	LESSON 18–19	LESSON 24–25		
FDR's New Deal			LESSON 21–22			
federal budget			LESSON 22			
House of Representatives		LESSON 12–14, 16	LESSON 19			
impeachment		LESSON 13–14	LESSON 19			
judicial branch		LESSON 12, 14	LESSON 18–19, 21			LESSON 39
legislative branch	LESSON 2, 6–9	LESSON 12–14, 17	LESSON 18, 22	LESSON 24–26		
negotiate and compromise		LESSON 13				
president as national leader		LESSON 17				
president's State of the Union address		LESSON 14				
preventing abuse of power	LESSON 2					
representative democracy	LESSON 3					
Senate		LESSON 12–14	LESSON 18–19			
separation of powers	LESSON 2	LESSON 13–14				
shared power	LESSON 2					
unconstitutional		LESSON 14				
U.S. Supreme Court	LESSON 3	LESSON 15	LESSON 18, 22	LESSON 23–27	LESSON 29, 33	
veto/veto override		LESSON 14				

Program 4_ Who Are Our Representatives and How Do We Choose Them?

We the People: The Citizen & the Constitution	UNIT ▲	▼1	▼2	▼3	▼4	▼5	▼6
	LESSON ▲	1–9	10–17	18–22	23–28	29–34	35–40
	TITLE ▲	What Are the Philosophical and Historical Foundations of the American Political System?	How Did the Framers Create the Constitution?	How Did the Values and Principles Embodied in the Constitution Shape American Institutions and Practices?	How Have the Protections of the Bill of Rights Been Developed and Expanded?	What Rights Does the Bill of Rights Protect?	What Are the Roles of the Citizen in American Democracy?
CONCEPT ▶							
checks and balances		LESSON 2, 6–7, 9	LESSON 12–17	LESSON 18–20	LESSON 23–28	LESSON 29–34	
constituents			LESSON 16				
influence of political parties				LESSON 20			
motivating voters							LESSON 35–36
political parties				LESSON 20	LESSON 27		
reasons to run for office		LESSON 1–3					LESSON 35–36
self-interest v. common good		LESSON 1–3					LESSON 35–36

143

Program 5_ How Do Representatives Work to Represent Us?

We the People: The Citizen & the Constitution	UNIT ▸ 1	2	3	4	5	6
LESSON ▸	1–9	10–17	18–22	23–28	29–34	35–40
TITLE ▸	What Are the Philosophical and Historical Foundations of the American Political System?	How Did the Framers Create the Constitution?	How Did the Values and Principles Embodied in the Constitution Shape American Institutions and Practices?	How Have the Protections of the Bill of Rights Been Developed and Expanded?	What Rights Does the Bill of Rights Protect?	What Are the Roles of the Citizen the Citizen in American Democracy?
CONCEPT ▸						
constituents		LESSON 16				
defining public interest	LESSON 2–3		LESSON 20			LESSON 36
The Federalist		LESSON 16–17				
legislative process		LESSON 13–14, 17				
majority rule v. common good	LESSON 2–3					LESSON 36
melding different constituencies	LESSON 3					LESSON 35
political parties			LESSON 20	LESSON 27		LESSON 36
proactive citizen						LESSON 36
representation and lawmaking		LESSON 17				
self-interest						LESSON 36
"special interest" groups	LESSON 2, 4		LESSON 20			
strengths and weaknesses of legislatures		LESSON 12–13, 17	LESSON 20			LESSON 35

Program 6_ What Are Citizens' Roles in Representative Democracy?

We the People: The Citizen & the Constitution

CONCEPT	UNIT ▸ 1 LESSON ▸ 1–9 TITLE ▸ What Are the Philosophical and Historical Foundations of the American Political System?	▸ 2 10–17 How Did the Framers Create the Constitution?	▸ 3 18–22 How Did the Values and Principles Embodied in the Constitution Shape American Institutions and Practices?	▸ 4 23–28 How Have the Protections of the Bill of Rights Been Developed and Expanded?	▸ 5 29–34 What Rights Does the Bill of Rights Protect?	▸ 6 35–40 What Are the Roles of the Citizen in American Democracy?
campaigns						
citizens' roles				LESSON 27		LESSON 35–36
Congress, the first branch of government		LESSON 15				
direct democracy	LESSON 2					
importance of youth involvement	LESSON 7	LESSON 16				LESSON 35
media and lobbying groups						LESSON 36–37
reelection provides accountability		LESSON 16		LESSON 27		
representative democracy	LESSON 3					
representatives as "voices of the people"	LESSON 1, 3					LESSON 36
republic	LESSON 3					
role of Congress		LESSON 12–14				

Acknowledgements

The Center for Civic Education wishes to acknowledge the following teachers for their assistance in the development of the Representative Democracy in America: Voices of the People video series:

Alvin Bell	Karen Ferris-Fernside	Julie Jacquish	Mark Oglesby
Ken Boesch	Tom Flaherty	Peter Kavouras	Lucinda Soule
Ed Cannady	Kevin Fox	Patti McMaster	Beth Ratway
Stephen Cianciolo	Melinda Harris	Jim Medina	Yvonne Rhodes
Roger Desrosiers	Rosie Heffernan	LeAnna Morse	Mary Smith
Abby Dupke	Amy Hennessy	Rique Ochoa	Katherin Sniffin

Expertise and Assistance

J. Jackson Barlow   PROFESSOR OF POLITICAL SCIENCE, JUNIATA COLLEGE, HUNTINGDON, PENNSYLVANIA

Sarah Binder   PROFESSOR OF POLITICAL SCIENCE, GEORGE WASHINGTON UNIVERSITY

Mark Cannon   FORMER STAFF DIRECTOR, COMMISSION ON THE BICENTENNIAL OF THE U.S. CONSTITUTION

Anthony Corrado   DANA PROFESSOR OF GOVERNMENT, COLBY COLLEGE, MAINE

Patrick Davidson   PATRICK DAVIDSON PRODUCTIONS

Roger Davidson   PROFESSOR EMERITUS OF GOVERNMENT AND POLITICS, UNIVERSITY OF MARYLAND

Lee H. Hamilton   DIRECTOR, THE CENTER ON CONGRESS AT INDIANA UNIVERSITY

Diane Hollern Harvey   DEPARTMENT OF PUBLIC AND INTERNATIONAL AFFAIRS, GEORGE MASON UNIVERSITY

Karl T. Kurtz   DIRECTOR, TRUST FOR REPRESENTATIVE DEMOCRACY/NATIONAL CONFERENCE OF STATE LEGISLATURES

Thomas Mann   SENIOR FELLOW, THE BROOKINGS INSTITUTION

Glenn Marcus   DOCUMENTARY FILMMAKER

Ken Nelson   ASSISTANT TO THE DIRECTOR, THE CENTER ON CONGRESS AT INDIANA UNIVERSITY

Ilona Nickels   FORMER CONGRESSIONAL RESEARCH SPECIALIST, CENTER ON CONGRESS AT INDIANA UNIVERSITY

Alan Rosenthal   PROFESSOR OF POLITICAL SCIENCE, EAGLETON INSTITUTE AT RUTGERS UNIVERSITY

Robert Schadler   AMERICAN FOREIGN POLICY COUNCIL, EDUCATIONAL ENRICHMENTS

Jayme Sokolow   PRESIDENT, THE DEVELOPMENT SOURCE, INC.

Center for Civic Education Staff Contributors

Charles N. Quigley   EXECUTIVE DIRECTOR

Tam Taylor   DIRECTOR, REPRESENTATIVE DEMOCRACY IN AMERICA

Margaret Branson   ASSOCIATE DIRECTOR

John Hale   ASSOCIATE DIRECTOR, ADMINISTRATION AND PROGRAM DEVELOPMENT

Mark Molli   ASSOCIATE DIRECTOR, GOVERNMENT RELATIONS

Charles Bahmueller   DIRECTOR, SPECIAL PROJECTS

Mark Gage   PRODUCTION EDITOR

Theresa Richard   EDITORIAL DIRECTOR

David Hargrove   EDITOR

Writers

Maria Gallo   DIRECTOR, SCHOOL VIOLENCE PREVENTION DEMONSTRATION PROGRAM

Dick Kean   MANAGING DIRECTOR OF PUBLICATION SERVICES

Design

Erin Breese, Mark Stritzel   COVER DESIGN

Mark Stritzel   INTERIOR DESIGN

Typography   AVENIR, AKZIDENZ GROTESQUE